Is Christ Divided?

A Biblical View of the Local Church–Para Church Anomaly

Dr. Felecia Rodgers

WESTBOW
PRESS
A DIVISION OF THOMAS NELSON

Unless otherwise indicated Scripture is taken from the New American Standard Bible, NASB, copyright 1960, 1962, 1963, 1968, 1971, 1972, 1973, 1975, 1977 by The Lockman Foundation. Used by permission.

WestBow Press books may be ordered through booksellers or by contacting:

WestBow Press
A Division of Thomas Nelson
1663 Liberty Drive
Bloomington, IN 47403
www.westbowpress.com
1-(866) 928-1240

ISBN: 978-1-4497-1737-7 (sc)
ISBN: 978-1-4497-1739-1 (hc)
ISBN: 978-1-4497-1738-4 (e)

Library of Congress Control Number: 2011931024

Printed in the United States of America

WestBow Press rev. date: 7/25/2011

I dedicate this effort in loving memory of my mother who inspired me to follow God's leading, taught me to have compassion for others and to pursue knowledge and understanding; to my dad, to my pastor and first lady, Reverend and Mrs. Arthur Hill who have been spiritual mentors, my brothers and sisters in Christ, family and friends.

He who speaks truth declares righteousness. Proverbs 12:17

CONTENTS

PREFACE

This text explores the controversy that exists between the local church and para-church organizations. It argues that the controversy continues because of perceptions surrounding the inherent roles and responsibilities of the local church. It also maintains that the assumed authority of the local church has displaced God's authority and the universality of the Church. These arguments are predicated upon biblical theology and the historical transformation regarding the New Testament Church. Analysis of scholarly literature reveals sociological, theological and historical perspectives which elucidate this discord underscoring the need for Christian leadership to explore and devise methodologies to create an intimate link between the two entities. The universal Church, biblically described as an interdependent system must strive for synergy to accomplish God's purpose. As it is written, "a kingdom divided against itself is laid waste; and a house divided against itself falls" (Luke 11:17). The church of the Bible is presented as a pattern of human life in marked contrast both to the values of secular culture and to the restrictive outlook that characterizes many religious groups. The Church is to be the manifestation of the philosophy to *love God and neighbor* exemplified in the life of Jesus who is the authority of every believer and demonstrated through the lives of the church. This research contributes to the body of Christian knowledge by presenting evidence of division and discord within the body of Christ, highlighting the rationale for antagonism between believers rather than the biblical rationale for unity and demonstrates the biblical perspective which supports cooperation between the local church and the para-church.

The combined and coordinated actions of the individual parts of the universal Church, specifically the local church and para-church, can achieve more than can be achieved acting independently. The catalyst for reconciliation is comprehension of the relational intricacies advocated in Scripture regarding the body of Christ with subsequent practical application of this Scriptural intent relevant to the church and para-church. Jesus on His quest to complete His assigned task presented the epitome of the para-church being autonomous, independent, receiving His directives from the ONE authority, guided by the Spirit in spite of fierce opposition; and battling disproportionate interpretations and incomprehensible hindrances which threatened foundational truths. The title para-church is an official recognition of defiance by the church which refutes para-church membership as being its representative and commissioned according to Scriptural edict (Mat. 28:19). Mutual esteem and cooperation is certainly preferable from both a spiritual and a worldly perspective, to antagonism; and shared convictions promote a more promising foundation for progression in the purposes of God than divisive, contradictory beliefs.

INTRODUCTION

The Bible states that there is only one Lord of the Church, Christ Jesus, and every believer comprises the Church as an elite group; "a peculiar people redeemed from all iniquity and purified unto God, zealous for good works" called disciples (Ti. 2:4). This fact has been distorted historically through divisive paradigm despite the evidence in Scripture which points to a community or family of believers regardless of geographical location, culture or political governance. The local church has not always been recognized as an institution, most literature identify it as a movement initiated by a meager constituency with minimal support much like any other organized venture seeking to transform the mindset of a society. According to the Bible, membership of the body of Christ is established by the profession of faith (Rom. 10: 9-10). The para-church comprises individuals who acknowledge allegiance to God in Christ often participating in local assemblies. As members of the body of Christ, the para-church has the conferred authority, by the Holy Spirit through being fundamentally interconnected as the Church in Christ. The controversy between the local church and para-church organizations is not substantiated in Scripture. The one unfailing truth regarding the Church throughout its inception is that God is the authority; the only authority who has given His vision of Kingdom building through the Holy Spirit to all who believe in Him. The biblical perspective supports cooperation between the church and the para-church.

Within the offices of Christian administration there exists a hierarchical arrangement which acknowledges authority and delineates lines of communication. This authority is given contingent upon a relationship with God and His intention (I Pet. 5:2-3). According to Scripture, every believer has the manifestation of the Spirit through gifting and these gifts are at the disposition of the Father (I Cor. 12:7). By this Spirit the motivation of the church and the para-church is an expression of "the love of God poured out into hearts" (Rom. 5:5; I John 4:19). As Scripture states, God has appointed apostles, prophets, teachers, miracles, gifts of healing, helps, administrations and various kinds of tongues in the Church (I Cor.12:28). These are roles and gifts with particular functions to accomplish the specific purposes of God. The para-church is a collaboration of faith-guided individuals engaging in ministry or mission through social welfare and evangelistic pursuits. They are often ecumenical by design, autonomous and may function independent of any one particular local church or specified religious association. Despite adversity the para-church attempts to be recognized as the universal Church engaged in evangelism and discipleship. Their efforts of building networks of independent organizations are an acknowledgement that the call of God is to converting the unsaved and sanctifying the converted. These associations concentrate primarily on evangelism and training for evangelism often with the incorporation of providing services to the nonbeliever. The bureaucracy of the local church and the obvious divisiveness of denominationalism, applies pressure on the para-church through disassociation and disenfranchisement. The dissension between the local church and the para-church must be reconciled for the advancement of God's kingdom. The often expressed controversy represents a departure from the fundamental edict in Scripture of one unbiased spiritual authority embracing every believer; and the biblically defined nature of the body of Christ in the purposes of God despite historicalness, traditionalism, denominationalism and any other divisive paradigm or hierarchical rule.

The discourse to follow is an exploration of history, denominationalism and church leadership perspective on mission motivations. It seeks to answer scripturally and historically basic philosophical tenets and historic transformations regarding the New Testament Church. Investigation of Scripture reveals the Church as a universal entity without separation due to culture, demographic or geographic location. The premise is the Word of God has established the Church characteristically under the authority of one God, as one body. It is, however, an institution which has undergone much development and change over the centuries. Its milieu has been plagued with an altering historical and philosophical climate and bureaucratic perspectives evoke an adversarial relationship within God's Church. Transformation is acknowledged as the emergence of multiple ecclesiologies, denominations and associations in response to varied human needs, perceptions and paradigms contemporarily dividing God's universal

Church into the local church and the para-church. Following the Protestant Reformation to the current epoch of post-modern Christianity, church leadership consigns the local church as the authority and principle medium of ministry and mission digressing the biblical concept of one Lord, one baptism, and one faith for the Church (Eph. 4:5). Based on philosophical assertions determined to explore the theological and biblical perspectives of the local church as a communal colony, the Spiritual inheritance of every believer, to discern the emergence of the para-church, to discover the local church perspective on the para-church and to analyze a theological basis advocating an integral relationship between the church and the para-church implicating the biblical perspective for cooperation between both organizations to alter any divisive paradigms.

This text examines these effects through the lens of the Bible considering some basic arguments of church leadership for separation. The goal is to answer the following questions within a theological and historical framework:

1. What are the characteristics of the local church and the para-church?
2. What reasons are cited for the para-church being under-supported by the local church?
3. What biblical values are reflected, supported and/or contradicted?
4. How important is the para-church to the reality of the church and the dissemination of the gospel message?

This endeavor does not distinguish cultural bias, racial, class or gender discrimination, denomination or religious affiliation. Neither does it include assessment of para-church organizations that are outside of the United States, under the authority of or supported by local church, denominational or church associations. It primarily considers the para-church ideology that has the Word of God as its foundation; and holds an ecumenical perspective and governance. Its purpose is to identify the integral relationship between the local church and the para-church to elicit support for collaboration.

Terminology

For the purpose of clarity the terms used will be defined:

The *church (lower case)* is defined as an institution, a local assembly of believers; separate gatherings of God's people in various locations, the edifice; "a spiritual or living temple" for worship, fellowship and witness.[1] In consideration of the centrality the church posits in the thinking of the newly converted early Christians, recognition is given to the description in the New Testament of what may be identified as a local church. The early believers met in houses rather than special sacred places. The Christians assembled for the apostle's teaching, fellowship, breaking of bread and prayer (Acts 2:42). They did not evangelize by inviting people to their meetings on Sunday but by witnessing to those with whom they would come in contact during the week or outside of the church. After conversion, people were brought into the fellowship and warmth of the local church to be nurtured and encouraged.

The term *Church (upper case)* represents the universal Church; "the called out ones," the entire body of believers everywhere. Grieg defines the Church as "a nation chosen by God, destined to be saved and to lead others to salvation as followers who would be a righteous remnant to found a new Israel" (Rom. 11:5; Gal. 3:29).[2]

A *Denomination* may be defined as a religious body having common name, doctrine and structure; "a group of Christians that have their own interpretation of aspects of Christian theology and their own organization."[3] Denominationalism, not a term in the Bible, is representative of diversity, multiple belief systems and personal philosophies although the fundamental premise of Scriptural framework may remain intact.

The *Para-church* may be recognized as a service provider organization or group having Christian philosophies, principles and standards as its foundation. Para-church organizations are defined as "voluntary, not-for-profit associations of Christians working outside denominational control to achieve some specific ministry or social service."[4]

A long history of intense conflict surrounding what constitutes the relationship between church and the para-church has been demonstrated in literature based on personal beliefs, theologies and ideologies; and noted as denominationalism and independent associations. The controversial nature of the relationship between the local church and the para-church relative to biblical foundations is distinguishable from the inclusivity the Bible postulates as proof of discipleship (John 13:35). The aim is to demonstrate that the Bible supports cooperation between the local church and the para-church. Multiple resources have been utilized to acquire scholarly literature including texts and journal articles that reveal and explain the various perspectives held regarding the para-church, the divisive relationship and the diverse points of view which advocate and oppose cooperation between the church and the para-church. Given the centrality of particular aspects to various outcomes in the life of Christianity it is essential to identify certain relevancy to the phenomenon being investigated. First, the Word of God is the final authority on what constitutes the Church. The Bible does not depict an ideal location, edifice or congregation; it presents a dynamic assemblage of diverse communities. Although there is no mention of para-church, the para-church has been in existence in some form for many centuries. The Bible provides evidence of efforts to make the gospel accessible to strangers, the commitment to world outreach and exhortation toward inculcating Christian teachings and values beginning with Jesus, the twelve disciples, Apostle Paul and countless others. It is plausible that the missionary movement of the New Testament involved an ecumenical ecclesiology, much like the para-church. "One must keep in mind the various levels of culture in which early Christianity moved: Palestinian Jews, Hellenistic Jews, Palestinian Jewish Christians, Hellenistic Jewish Christians; and Greek or non-Jewish Christians, all living in the midst of a pagan society."[5] According to David Stanley, "members of the local church were faced with addressing themselves to the Greek public of their day, not only to narrate the gospel message but to express essentially Christian concepts" through word and deed.[6] The Bible is the ultimate standard for critical evaluation of the purposes and function of the local church.

Second, the integrality of the church and the para-church is espoused by the Word of God as the one universal Church. The New Testament Church is identified as one universal body corporately interwoven; individually or collectively engaged in Christ for the ministry of restoring the world to God. The Scripture contends that God does not dwell in "temples made with hands" but in human temples established as a "Spiritual house" (Acts 17:24; I Pet. 2:5). The church is the people of God in whom the Spirit of God dwells. Both the local church and the para-church are assemblies and institutions of the people of God. Divisive philosophical and theological perspectives presents as separation within the body of Christ, therefore, para-church organizations are considered the establishment of abnormal institutions described as counterfeit "cooperative endeavors having non-hierarchal forms of government."[7] Wilmer et al. describes the para-church as "religion gone entrepreneurial" yet perceives it as God "expanding his work by enlarging the boundaries of Christian ministry."[8] Affirming the biblical perspective of support for cooperation between the church and the para-church, Stackhouse asserts that the church having the biblically mandated responsibility of "equipping the saints means empowerment of individuals for God's service, the acceptance of leadership in both organizations as co-laborers together sharing resources for the common cause and contributing to efforts of each institution (Eph. 4:12)."[9] Accordingly he states that, "the New Testament teaches that all members are important, expected to serve and should be honored as they do so; and that various gifts and roles are to edify the body, to extend Christ's mission of service to the world and bring honor to God."[10] He affirms that as members of the universal Church through diverse congregations the para-church can serve usefully.[11] Contrary to the tenet held by many that the para- church is *out of order* and in opposition to the local church, the reality is that the para-church, founded on the principles of the gospel and the local church have distinct, but integrative roles and responsibilities in God's commission.

Although some scholars note an inherent association between the church and the para-church, others assert that the para-church has established itself outside of the traditional church and its associated organizational structures; and therefore, is incongruent. It has been argued that the debate is over the content of Christianity, the essence of the church and *The Truth*. John Hammet contends that the para- church must honor and defer to the local church since the para-church is justifiably subordinate according to theological argument.[12] It is depicted by its opposition as commercialism because of its autonomy, innovative and entrepreneurial style. Charry contends that the para- church is befitting of American consumerism with its emphasis on personal religiosity rather than corporate soteriology (soul-saving).[13] None of these opponents resolve to identify the para-church as the body of Christ in complimentary endeavors furthering God's kingdom. Although recognizing the positive aspects of the para-church; defining it as organizations with "an apparent Christian character and purpose," it is observed as a fragmented group of Christians with "tunnel vision."[14] There is the contention, quite insulting in fact, that apart from any particular denomination or congregation the para-church "is often doing what churches cannot, are not doing or are not doing well."[15] Scripture attests that God can attain His purposes through whatever means that He deems appropriate. The Bible never extols a specific building or group but presents each church as one unified body. This necessitates a challenge for the local churches and denominational associations to avert divisiveness through camaraderie and communication and to maintain Christ's vision as the objective that energizes the mission of "the diverse stakeholders."[16]

Third, the Word of God explains the expected purpose of the church and the para-church. The biblical perspective distinguishes the local church as a gathering of believers for protection, nourishing, safety and learning. Following development as disciples through the church a cyclical pattern emerges. Christians are instructed to go out among the nations, make disciples and teach what matters to God which is the ingathering of believers for protection, nourishing, safety and learning (Matt. 28: 19-20; Mark 12:10). Every member of the body of Christ, as the church and the *branded* para-church is required to carry God's message in accordance to His commission (Rom.10:15). The varied exegetical and hermeneutical frameworks demonstrated within Christianity pose difficulty in analysis of this issue. Being divinely inspired, Scripture must mean what it has always meant (II Tim. 3:16). D. A. Carson writes, "to treat some element of biblical theology as if it existed in isolation seriously distorts the whole picture."[17] Scripture requires that every believer be as one peaceably (Rom. 12:1-18). However, explications and interpretations abound, and debate, suspicion, and controversy are inherent to biblical comprehension. According to Yarchin, "for as long as the Bible has been read, people have interpreted it at many different levels of sophistication and toward different purposes for understanding and application."[18] Therefore, in hermeneutics and modernity the universal Church becomes divided and this is accepted as fact because every possibility is relevant to analysis. This highlights the complexity of the problem of employing theological and historical exegesis specific to the relevance of the para-church as inherent to the local church. Any solution presented may be determined to be an incomplete solution since there may be areas not chosen for analysis. Clergy, philosophers, and theologians, each relying upon their particular versions of exegesis and hermeneutics, probe and expound on the Hebrew Scriptures, the New Testament and other ancient texts to make sense of the world. The message of Scripture is "God is love, the fruit of the Spirit is love and loving one another is proof we are His children" (Gal. 5:22; I John 4:7). Christ did not come into the world to condemn it, but that through Him all who believe are saved (John 3:17) Is Christ divided? Carson contends that "to approach the Bible correctly it is important to know something of the God who stands behind it."[19] The Bible explicates that the church and the para-church have kinship through one Holy Spirit affirming that the biblical perspective supports cooperation between the church and the para-church.

Fourth, the Word of God presents evidence sufficient to confirm the hypothesis that the biblical perspective supports cooperation between the church and the para-church. Everyone who believes are "called according to God's purpose" as disciples in the Great Commission and included among a "royal priesthood" (Rom. 8:28; Matt. 28:19-20; I Pet. 2:9). God reveals through Scripture that He is transcendental yet, personal and communal. He does not condone favoritism and exalts humility. The Bible rebukes "a faith that exhibits an attitude of personal favoritism" (James 2:1; NAS). Piety, arrogance, self-centeredness and partiality are confronted in the Bible on many levels. Jesus asserts that anyone doing good deeds in His name cannot deny the Christ and should not be encumbered (Mark 3:39). Peter was instructed not to call unclean what God says is clean and Paul wrote questioning judgment of another man's servant (Acts 10:15; Rom. 14:4). Evidence exists throughout Scripture emphasizing the depth and breadth of God's sovereign election and His intention toward indivisible love universally among brethren. In the Gospel of Mark the ninth chapter, the disciples disclose feelings of apprehension regarding a man who healed in Jesus' name and was not a member of the elect group of disciples. They appear more concerned with the identity of their own select group than in helping to free those troubled by demons (Mark 9: 38). Their issues may be similar to those of the local church or association who argue that the para-church which does not affiliate with a specific denomination, does not involve the kind of people with whom they are used to associating; doesn't do the things the way they are accustomed to doing them and that the local church, denomination or association won't get the recognition.

Lastly, conclusions ascertained from this undertaking have worth to the vitality of Christianity, elevating unity in the body of Christ to its respective Scripturally-advocated position which will profoundly affect multitudes of prospective onlookers perhaps effecting their transformation. The predicament expressed between the two institutions is exacerbated by antagonism instead of the preferred desire for healing and recovery; and an economic agenda has an incapacitating consequence relative to reconciliation or acknowledgement on the part of the local church; causing further or continued division. Without reconciliation to God and His purpose, no culture or system within a culture will operate flawlessly; "and if a kingdom is divided against itself, that kingdom cannot stand. And if a *Church* is divided against itself, that *Church* will not be able to stand" (Mark 3:24-25, *emphasis added*). In Scripture it has been concluded that there are distinctions of roles though they are uniquely fashioned together, acknowledging diversity and the aspiration for universality according to the will of God (I Cor. 12). Some eat meat, some recognize a day; others consider all the same and this should not cause division but, as the body of Christ, the Word of God sanctions laboring together for a common purpose (Rom.14). Scripture admonishes: "do all things to the glory of God" (I Cor. 10:31). Is Christ divided?

CHAPTER 1

THE CHURCH AS A COMMUNAL COLONY

The focal point of community and learning in religious circles has been a meeting place. The common meeting place, though called by many names: synagogue, mosque, church is the location where individuals meet to engage in practices of mutual consent and commonality. The local church is a community which presents the perspective of individuals organized around common values and social cohesion within a shared geographical location. As a community its identity is shaped by common intent, belief, resources, preferences, needs and risks. The church has been established throughout the world as a community within a community assenting to an *in the world but not of the world* stance, having external and internal governance and allegiance. These communities are often developed in response to the Holy Spirit, the preaching of the gospel and the perceived relationship toward the preacher or Christian leadership. The church is a congregation of Christian believers who is the universal Church, the Body of Christ, acknowledging the gospel message through faith and accepting the Bible as the truth. The inculcation of truth may be observed by the relational aspects expressed in communion with the Lord and His body of believers. The Bible explicates that beyond the initial impetus as a place of worship and for tithing and charitable giving; the community of believers, the local church assembling together, promotes faithful witness to the gospel and is required to extend teaching and support along the believer's earthly sojourn. The church has been established by God to be a functional institution enabling every believer to engage in the Great

Commission. The biblical perspective supports the local church having the God-ordained responsibility to develop each member to facilitate evangelism and discipleship which is identified as the focus of the parachurch. Consequently, cooperation between the local church and parachurch, as institutions formed by the universal Church each individually comprised of the community of believers, is espoused in Scripture.

A Geographic Identity

The Bible references various congregations of believers which are identified regionally such as the churches at Ephesus, Corinth, Galatia, Thessalonica and Jerusalem. These localities were established as organized communal colonies enabling the spiritual community to grow in knowledge, understanding and wisdom; to engage in communal support and to worship God. A colony may be defined as a group of newly located and newly established individuals who maintain the original establishment's governance as its foundation. The new settlement remains dependent and incorporates foundational messages and a system of beliefs. The church as a communal colony conveys the universality of biblical truths of the original membership into each region and every geographical relocation. The emphasis is that of unity in perspective, philosophy and practice under the governance of its Founder. The communal nature of the church is expressed when Jesus being confronted regarding the Mosaic Law is required to present that precept which is the most important for the inquiring Jewish leadership. Identification with the existing religious community, the chosen nation of Israel, was obvious to the questioning Jewish nation when Jesus established that the same legal understanding and responsibility as under the Mosaic Law was mandated through the covenant of Grace; to love the Lord God with all of the heart, mind and soul and each other as ourselves (Deut 6:5; Matt.22:37). The existence of the communal colony is further translated to the universal Church as the apostles promote the need for each congregation of believers to be of like-minds, though separated by distance (Phil. 2:2-1).

Following acceptance of Jesus Christ as personal savior and Lord, a local church affords opportunity for unity with other believers as an assembly of the body of Christ to grow in spiritual knowledge and wisdom. Spiritual gifts are manifested to nurture and enable reproduction. According to the text, *Why Church Matters*, the Church's purpose, goal or orientation is not a conscious choice, although the individual is directed to act by virtue of an identity as a born again believer.[1] "It is something we receive that we are free to choose only as God enables us."[2] The local church is directed as a body of believers to "declare what can only be known by the gift of knowledge given through faith to each believer in Jesus Christ; and the mission is to witness of the kingdom by being disciples and making disciples."[3] The local church as the communal colony, a component of the universal Church, has been given its purpose by God and that purpose is to proclaim the Excellencies of God (I Pet. 2:9-10).

A Familial Identity

In the New Testament, the local church as a communal colony may be compared to a family; as families usually congregate together based on the intimacy of similarity. Denominationalism confers assembly based on similarity. It is defined in the text, *Bible Answers for Almost All Your Questions,* as an individual church or grouping of churches with similar doctrinal beliefs, traditions and historical backgrounds being bound organically to establish corporately, ministry unattainable separately through the sharing of the same goals including the desire for fellowship together.[4] However, membership in Christ's Church affords that which is universally inclusive and not separated by denominationalism or doctrinal perspective. The biblical contention regarding specifically identifying churches or individuals by having labels of entitlement as from God is rebuked as divisive (I Cor. 1:12). There is no mention in God's word of denominations such as Baptists, Anglicans, Methodists, Presbyterians, Pentecostals or Catholics. Individual assemblies were identified by their geographical location. Still, denominationalism is a form of community and can be an expression of family relationship. Referencing denominationalism and the church affords the division of a religious group into subgroups specific to commonality in name, religious tradition and cultural-social identity. Denominationalism does not focus solely on belief and curriculum. The many different denominations are often divided by doctrinal interpretation, practice or methodology. It maintains its community by nurturing a distinctive pattern of religiosity and traditions as the force which binds them together. Much like a colony, most are governed by a centralized association, fellowships or conventions. Although denominations, recognizably a community of believers have become one of the largest expressions of organized Christianity beyond the level of the congregation, there is no biblical basis for division in the body of Christ, local or universal.

To further emphasize the communal and familial aspect of the local church in Scripture, cultural and religious composition was of no consequence to the dissemination of the gospel. The geographical distribution of early Christianity was such that many externalities affected the development of the early church: in Palestine the church was predominately Jewish, though it included Samaritans; the church at Antioch contained Jews and Gentiles, the church of Ephesus was engulfed by Greek customs; Philippi was a Roman colony; the church at Corinth was multi-ethnic, and the church at Colossae comprised Jewish and Hellenistic elements.[5] However, Paul could write a letter to the Christians meeting in the various places throughout Rome, Greece or Galatia with every assurance that all who were established under one authority would receive its message. Consequently, the local church as a communal colony demonstrating a family relationship involves the contribution of its members, the assembling together for worship and the equipping of saints is important to God's redemptive plan for mankind and the Bible supports solidarity through the gospel.

A Spiritual Identity

In worship, the believer is exhorted to delight in God (Psalm 16:11; Acts 2:46). The Book of Revelation displays a glimpse into heaven where there is a great assembly of saints who worship "the Lamb that was slain" (5:12). The believer is summoned to seek personal and communal relationship with God and fellow believers (Heb.10:22; James 4:8). Finally, worship allows unbelievers to experience God's presence. Paul exhorted the Church at Corinthians to be sure that they considered the presence of outsiders and to ensure that Christians worshipped in understandable ways (1 Corinthians 14:23). Thus allowing unbelievers the opportunity to recognize that "God is really among you" affording affirmation of Him (1 Corinthians 14:25).

The Bible asserts that believers must "stir up one another to love and good works; not forsaking the assembling together" (Heb.10:24-25). The church as a communal colony has been appointed Christian leadership for teaching, training, correcting and enabling the processes of God to be manifested. Each member within the body of Christ has responsibility assigned according to the faith that has been given. According to Brackney, "It is obvious among persons with heightened religious interest that involvement and participation in a religious act or association is fundamental to their religious affections."[6] The communal colony has biblical reference and a Holy Spirit directive for its policy and as a community is required to perform the various mandates to fulfill the individual promptings that are portions of a master plan. James writes, "Show me your faith apart from works and I will show you my faith by my works" (2:18) The assertion is that the community of faithful collectively and individually demonstrates identification as believers through behaviors and attitudes. This depicts the need for a social network and participatory activities which receive their meaning as a part of the internal and external conceptual relationship of the communal colony. A relevant component of the local church is its proclivity toward outward expressions of worship indicative of a communal colony having relationship with God through submission and acknowledging that His kingly reign has arrived. The two-fold ministry given by Jesus to the universal Church and to be made manifest through the local church is to "learn of me and make disciples," suggesting the enterprising, ordained development of missions which may be identified contemporarily as the para-church (Mat. 11:29; 28:19-20).

Jesus gathered His followers into a community to receive justification through faith and restoration through God's promise, securing identification with Jesus and the Father. Community was the essence of Jesus' earthly ministry (John 17:21). Since individually and collectively the Church is one in Christ and the church and para-church are participants as the body of believers, there should be no hostility to individual liberty and cooperation is reasonable. Having been set apart and provided revelation each member of the body is commanded to remain connected to Christ and to "bear much fruit" to the glory of the Father, thereby exhibiting discipleship and devotion (John 15:4-5, 8). Recognition and acceptance as God's chosen people facilitated the preservation of the communal colony even in the wake of the Diaspora. The children of Israel, though separated from the larger group still maintained their identity even in foreign lands. Although their services were performed in a hostile environment apart from the original assembly, Daniel and the other Hebrew boys were not discouraged from their affiliation with their foundational beliefs and obedience to God (Dan. 1-3). Scripture attests to individuals such as Abraham, Samson, Moses and Esther who as representatives of a communal colony demonstrated individual liberty expressed as obedience to a specific Spiritual call, where by faith and justified through actions they obtained the promises of God (Gen. 12:1-4; Ex. 4; Esther 4:8, 12-16;18; Judg. 13:5, 18-20). According to biblical accounts, originating from a communal colony of believers where spiritual knowledge and growth is acquired, God gave instruction through prophets, teachers and spiritual leaders so believers would grow in knowledge, skill, and discernment to fulfill the divine purposes of God.

BIBLICAL CHURCH HISTORY

The Old Testament affirms the importance of the assembly of those that God has called or chosen to worship Him. It communicates the portrayal and revelation of God's ideal and His covenant. Covenant Theology promotes a bond which creates a consistent conceptual relationship. This covenant is an implied, unilaterally established relational bond encompassing the issues of life and death for every believer. The phenomenon of the divine covenant of grace or treaty between God and man is evident during Old and New Testament periods. While the eternal covenant was made between the Father and the Son (Genesis 1:26), the covenant of grace is made between God and man (John 3:16). Believers are in covenant relationship with God beginning with Adam through Christ. For example, the Old Testament depicts the Sinaitic Covenant, often named the Mosaic Covenant, which began within the historical context of God's covenantal relationship with a nation in community to be expressed as God's everlasting heavenly kingdom (James 2:5). The Sinaitic Covenant was not purposed to instill or encourage a spirit of haughtiness, but to establish an everlasting priesthood of believers foreshadowing the future kingdom's subjection to the will of God (I Peter 2:9). The New Testament is so named to contrast it with the previously represented testament or Old Testament. Following many centuries of silence between God and the prophets, the New Testament of the Bible emerges, testifying and reaffirming God's sovereignty and love for mankind. Within this covenantal message Jesus presented the conception of a new Israel. The Messianic Covenant often identified as the New Covenant is the consummation of previous historical covenants or the series of covenantal systems. This covenant was different from its predecessors as it did not require circumcision of the flesh, laws written in stone or ceremonial rituals. It abolished and fulfilled these temporal elements and completed the cycle of the covenantal revelation (Matthew 5:17). Although processes, structure, formulation, categories and particular details of the covenant may vary, God's bond with His people ultimately unites to a single communal relationship having its expression throughout myriad assemblies of the community of believers.

The Old Testament Ecclesia

In the Old Testament ecclesia, the affirmation of a particular doctrine and the denial of another are seen within each assembly. The populous of the people of God assembled to engage in practices which defined its group identity. Assembling together professes a relationship of obligation and responsibility to one another. The systemic component of the Judaism ecclesia provides the intricacies of the framework afforded the Old Testament assembly. In Scripture each member is presented as endowed with all that is necessary to be substantially Jewish: irrevocably chosen by the power of God and distinguished to be uncompromisingly in pursuit of holiness. Accordingly in the Old Testament ecclesia, "differentiation among the Gentile converts rarely, if ever, made a difference in systemic decision making."[7] The Jewish system confirms a communal colony as the ecclesia of the Old Testament imparts a Jewish nation with "an autonomy and meaning all their own, so that each complex component formed a microcosm of the whole."[8] In Genesis 28:22, Jacob set up a stone as a pillar and called it *Beth El*, "God's house." [9] Paul references this in his writings to Timothy, when he describes God's house as the church, using the Greek word ecclesia (1 Tim. 3:15). Ecclesia is a Greek word for assembly; the called out ones and translated as church in the New Testament. *Strong's Concordance* defines it as being called out.[10] It is translated convocation, and assembly in Ex. 12:16; Isa. 1:13; Neh. 8:8. In the Book of Nehemiah, chapter eight verses 1-12, we are provided with examples of the kind of activities in which the ecclesia engaged when it convened:

- To gather together as one
- To read the Word of God
- To worship God
- To expound the Word of God
- To teach according to the Word of God
- To receive and express joy in understanding the Word of God

The Book of Nehemiah presents the covenant renewal and spiritual restoration of the Jewish community following dispersion. It provides the evidence that the Old Testament ecclesia was an assembly "filled with people having experienced God's redemption and renewal, revealing themselves as a communal colony of people to whom the law of God has been entrusted and recognizing their dependence on Him are committed to a life of faithful obedience."[11]

Synagogue in Greek means a place for coming together or a meeting place resembling a Christian church service. Although its origination is not mentioned in the Old Testament, synagogues probably originated during the exile in Babylon as meetings of the people to hear the inspired writings and to pray.[12] Separated from Jerusalem and their temple, the exiles established synagogues to facilitate assembling the communal colony of believers to enable the preserving of their faith and a place for public worship. The earliest synagogues were likely to have been living rooms or courtyards. As time passed and persecution lessened, people constructed special places for their meetings. Synagogues became centers of learning and worship, an expression of the Jewish people's interrelationship, ardent faith and love of God. By the time of Jesus' earthly visit, many Jewish communities, throughout the Roman world, had its synagogue. It became the pivot of the Jewish community. Worship within a synagogue, though variant due to geographical location was an important visible expression of Judaism, and the chief means of uniting the Jews scattered throughout the world. As a means of crystallizing the community of believers, the synagogue, is a most important feature of the Jewish communal colony, representative of the Old Testament Ecclesia which is a precursor of the New Testament Ecclesia, the inception of Christianity and the institution of the local church.

In the Old Testament narrative illustration of Noah and the ark, Scripture conceivably provides a symbolic reference to Jesus and His Church. According to the Book of Genesis, eventually people spread throughout the earth after God sent Adam and Eve out from the Garden of Eden. However, these people were so wicked that God decided to rid the earth of them. In accordance with God's standards, Noah was one man among the multitude who was decidedly righteous and upright. The Lord spoke only to Noah, readying him for the day of reckoning and acknowledgement of his obedience. People gathered to ridicule, chastise and question Noah's state of mind, but, as God commanded, Noah built a huge boat with three levels and a roof; places to store and prepare food, to sleep, sustain and thrive. Into the ark came every kind of male and female beast, along with Noah's wife, three sons and their wives. All found safety inside of the ark as rain fell heavily upon the earth for forty days and nights covering every valley and mountain from sight. After the tumultuous storm, land was revealed. Noah and his family, "blessed" by God, were instructed to be *fruitful and multiply* (Gen. 6-9).

Noah is often analogized as a type of Jesus, the Savior; his family and all those that came may be representative of the church. The ark is the tabernacle, the dwelling place of God for the church, the community of believers. It is portrayed as a place where the elect finds refuge, nourishing, learning and protection; the nonbelievers remained on the outside. Safe from life's storms, following restoration, spiritual renewal and growth, though some may have stayed with the ark, the community of believers was enabled to venture away from the ark on God's mission. This representation suggests that as the whole assembly, the faithful are to gather together in worship before God in whatever local community they might actually be found. All community members are heirs of a great tradition stretching backward to the call of Abraham. The church and the para-church constitutes every believer entering into the covenant inheritance of the universal community who, facilitated by gifted representatives of Jesus, receive protection, nourishing, safety, spiritual growth and direction and once strengthened are instructed to go out among the diverse populous and make disciples illustrative of biblical support for cooperation between the church and the para-church (Mat. 28: 19-20; Mark 12:10).[13] In the New Testament, through His teachings and actions, Jesus proposed the New Testament ecclesia to gather this new community of disciples who were to impart their knowledge to the world that none would be forever separated from relationship with Him (II Pet. 3:9).

The New Testament Ecclesia

The New Testament Ecclesia espouses that God is revisiting His covenantal relationship with His elect. The New Testament of the Bible comprises books which substantiates God's covenantal love. The terms testament and covenant are often used interchangeably. Testament is defined as a will or covenant and covenant means a spiritual agreement originating from the Greek word diatheke.[14] Christian Scriptures, therefore, constitute a pact, alliance or agreement between God and His people. Covenant Theology establishes that although the Old Testament communal colony of believers, the Nation of Israel, failed in fulfilling its covenantal responsibilities, God repeatedly provided opportunity for reconciliation. The prophet Jeremiah foretold of the Lord's new covenant with His ecclesia that would enable the community of believers to keep this final agreement (31:33). Scripture attests that God will not fail in His purpose which is to establish a great people and a great nation to glorify His name (John 11: 50, 52; Heb. 8:10). Jesus is the ultimate sacrifice and

9

unlike the sacrifices of the old covenant, which made nothing perfect, the sacrifices of Jesus is able to fulfill this final covenant and thereby save completely those who come to God through Him (Heb. 7:19, 25; 9). As is customary to any agreement or promise there are criteria to be followed, therefore, despite the assurance of covenant stipulations God's covenant of eternal life has conditional aspects of godly repentance and obedience. Flew writes that the New Testament ecclesia "birthed the conception of the universal Church" because the body of believers; the Jewish Church, was already in existence and Christ's fulfillment of the covenantal agreement shaped a "purged and reconstituted Israel" to present a new ecclesiastical kingdom.[15]

Prior to the arrival of Jesus, "Judaism had already become sharply divided and quite variegated with a whole Diaspora culture developing in various parts of the ancient world."[16] Jesus confronted Israel's teachings and beliefs, challenging a "reappraisal of the nation's spiritual life and the ancient covenant between God and Israel" which He extended to all of mankind.[17] Scripture reports that the man-made temple, though having a venerated position in the life of the believer should not take precedence over Jesus who directs the church and identified himself as the true temple (Mat. 8:4; John 2:19-22; Mk. 15:58). The Jewish Law, synagogues, temple and Christian Churches were outward expressions of the relationship between God and mankind. Stephen overtly challenged the eminence of the temple and ceremonial law (Acts 7). He spoke to prepare the masses for the changes in Judaic traditions that had arrived which presented initially as "the estrangement and distinction of God's new community from the traditional people of God" and he was stoned.[18] The New Testament ecclesia determined that the rituals and traditions of the temple were no longer to have primacy in the believing community. Based on biblical record the incontrovertible conclusion is that God's relationship with humanity predates buildings, laws, rituals and traditions. The New Testament is the foundational message for the Church which is the eternal covenant promise God made "before the foundation of the world" (I Pet.2:20). This covenant of Grace is to all believers without classification.

The Bible attests that the statement *all believers* comprises the Jewish and the Gentile communities of the world. Believers not bound by denominationalism, tradition or physical walls, who are commissioned and called to task as workmen of God, knowledgeable representatives of the New Testament ecclesia and commissioned to work through the local church and para-church institutions, being likewise communal colony constituents (II Tim. 2:15). The commission of the constituency is expressed in the freedom of the Holy Spirit which goes where God wills (John 3:8). Scripture proposes a requisite establishment of order to maintain community and therefore administers Christian leadership and guidance to equip the saints as they "go" outside of the confines and sanctity of the local church to do the work of the Lord according to the plan and call of God (Jer. 29:11; Mat. 28:19; Prov. 3:5-6). God is the centrality of the covenant relationship with everyone that believes, as promised through the Gospel; and dispersal of the gospel message throughout humankind is to be carried out by the body of Christ. To advance the purposes of God, Paul's demonstrated strategy was to meet initially in the synagogues utilizing his cultural heritage and theological prowess to advance the Gospel. Paul, an apostle, under the authority of God; not a specific local assembly and directed by the Holy Spirit, is an example of one united under the New Testament ecclesia who sought to persuade the Jewish communal colony who was influenced by various traditions, religious hostilities, and cultural nuances, of the reaffirmation of God's covenant with a chosen people comprising both Jews and Gentiles.

The New Testament Christian church is an expansion on the relationship under the old covenant. As a result of Paul's missionary journeys disseminating the message of grace and community, institution of the Christian Church as a new communal colony flourished although there were identified "problems caused by the inclusion of Gentiles, in what began as a movement within Judaism."[19] This aspect further elucidates the attendance in the ecclesia as specific to a community of believers; although inquirers were ever-present. Porter states that "the exclusive and honored title of Israel, its divine election as God's people, is now appropriated and applied to the flock of Christ, the community of the disciples of Christ," the Christian Church.[20] The covenant of Grace indicates that the people of God could not be limited by geographical boundaries, national, cultural, political or social inhibitions (Mat. 8:10-13; Luke. 13:29-30). Jesus stressed an element of exclusion for the unrepentant, but anyone with a faithful and repentant heart, were considered sons and daughters of the kingdom with inclusion in the New Testament ecclesia. In Romans, 9:22-26, Paul establishes that the new community of God's people was prophesied in Hosea: "I will call those who are not My people, My people" (2:23). This new covenant, after the Sinaitic Covenant having been brought to fruition forged its way through the words and deeds of the apostles who, guided by the Holy Spirit presented the formulation of the New Testament ecclesia. Paul's letters to the Jews and Gentiles were to be a catalyst for all believers and the narrative for the establishment of the universal Church of God having its expression in numerous settings, while maintaining its distinctive identity as the meeting place facilitating spiritual nurture and growth for the people of God.

EARLY CHURCH HISTORY

The universal Church may be defined as the worldwide body of believers chosen by God to enter into a relationship through Jesus and developed as a result of His teachings and sovereignty. It is a collective term for all the people of God. The local church is an assembly of believers gathering together in one locality for the purpose of worshipping God, Spiritual growth and learning and bearing witness to the good news of Jesus Christ. Both the local church and the universal Church exist for God as they are fundamentally the same. In Ephesians, chapter 5 it states that the church is under the authority of Christ and required to depend on this authority for sanctification through refinement by the Word of God and the presence and receipt of the Holy Spirit (23-27). The analogy is a bride or marriage union characterized by the receipt of love, nourishment and cherishing from the groom or husband. This is indicative of the established relational aspects of the body of believers as a community with God and having its existence reinforced through this relationship which has developed out of faith in Jesus. Jesus' primary call was to "follow me" and "come to me" (Mat. 4:19; 11:28). The authority to preach, teach, rebuke, correct, exhort and to perform healings and other miraculous works was afforded to Him by God. Jesus taught many things, particularly emphasizing the kingdom of God and eternal life for believers. He explained conduct, methodology and philosophy for the children of God, who are to be representatives of God. Jesus appointed twelve individuals for specific tasks and to have specialized knowledge, however, many were followers. These followers met regularly, inquired of His wisdom, dined with Him and witnessed His many signs and wonders. There were many besides the twelve who were in his company daily, acquiring and expending what was needed to be His disciple. Jesus said that His ministry was for the lost chosen people (Matt. 15:24). He purposed to restore the elect to the community of faith. His efforts to correct ideologies and misconceptions in the growing assembly were exhaustive. One example was when He drove away the merchants from the temple. The merchants' purpose and practice may have been a reasonable method of adherence to laws and customs, but the intent of religiosity which became burdensome, maliciousness, the practice impeded the Gentile's worship and as a scourge to divine sensibilities required redress (Matt. 21:12-13). The underlying message is that Jesus has undeniable lordship over the temple and the relationship between God and His elect.

"The paradox" of the people of the original covenant "lies in the ambivalence of their obedience to a law which culminated in the love of God and in the exclusivism of circumcision, Sabbath and sectarianism without which they would never have preserved their identity."[21] Jesus denounced adherence to laws and traditions that inhibit obedience to the standards and the will of God; that inferred domination or ill to the brethren and prohibited individual expression of worship. He ushered in the inauguration for all people to worship God "in spirit and in truth" (John 4:23-24). Additional examples of Jesus' efforts to correct ideologies and misconceptions in His plan to restore the elect were demonstrated through His conversation during meetings with Nicodemus and the Canaanite woman. Nicodemus, who had been counted as one of God's chosen according to Judaism, was a Pharisee, a member of an elite religious group and therefore, well acquainted with Jewish teachings. Nicodemus approached Jesus for inquiry. Jesus emphasized that even though the chosen people of Israel held the office of authority within the assembly, they did not have the position of relationship. Alternatively, a Canaanite woman seeking remedy for her child conceded her faith in Jesus and her desire for relational consideration (John 3:1-3; Matt. 15:22-28). She had been chosen by God, as Jesus states: "no one can come to me unless the Father who sent me draws him (John 6:44)." Knowing the depth of her conviction and although not a customary representative of the elect, Jesus allowed the woman's acceptance into the New Testament ecclesia. Both examples demonstrate that the New Testament ecclesia was not to be characterized by governance which thwarted individual expressions of faith. Christ as the cornerstone and teacher of the church, presents its function as one of deliverance and guidance in truth without focus on position, power, class or culture. In each instance, the goal was conversion, following repentance. Recovery of the elect necessitated Spiritual regeneration relinquishing personal pride and self-reliance to afford participation in the purposed eternal communal family of God. Jesus presents a new beginning to contrast the old and a new ecclesia which was different from the historical religious and secular worlds with its customs, traditions, ideologies and governance; all of which causes division. The goal was for God's New Testament people to advance an observable transformation of unity in the spirit that would translate into a new assembly, the Church.

In the Church Every Believer is a Disciple

Tradition suggests that membership of a local church requires baptism in the Spirit of God and water as the accompanying demonstration by which believers enter into union with Christ, His communal colony and become disciples. Disciple means learner; one who follows another's teachings.[22] The word is used for disciples of Jesus as an expression for the Jewish nation who became Jesus' adherents and is currently utilized to identify everyone who professes that they are children of God. The New Testament Scripture enforces disciple-making. The accomplishments of the early church disciples provide the evidence that the Bible does not specify exclusivity by laity or clergy, whether it should be performed individually or corporately; as part of a local community or without. It simply advocates that it is the requirement of every believer to become a disciple and to develop others as disciples. Disciples are often spoken of as imitators. They are identified as those persons who have learned specific characteristics and principles from another and who are maintaining them recognizably as under the auspices of the instructing individual. The biblical portrait of a disciple of Christ is evidenced by demonstrations of teaching, praying and acknowledging the divine authority of God in daily life. The biblical call is to surrender of one's life, to submit to Divine rule and to embrace struggle as the natural consequence of discipleship in a world that is in rebellion against the Word of God.[23] The effectiveness of discipleship in Christ is prefaced by good stewardship, service, compassion and spirit-driven wisdom culminating as identifiable behaviors and attitudes. The Bible displays a profound portrayal of mankind's eternal destiny. Its emphasis on eternal life and God's Kingdom contends that all believers will have to give an account as disciples of Christ. The development of the disciple of Christ requires more than casual consideration. The innate qualities that comprise godly discipleship necessitate the exorbitant expenditure of every believer to renounce self. It is established and maintained by a faithful, habitual commune and assembly with God. This is what occurred with the original disciples and was influential to the development of the early church.

The Supreme Teacher revealed to His disciples God's plan for the New Testament ecclesia. He provided the experience of an assembly of faithful witnesses and concurred that: "upon this rock, I will build my

Church" in preparation for one united kingdom of God having the same Lord (Mat.16: 17-18). The community of disciples was expected by its teacher to be interdependent, mutually supportive and disciplined (Luke 22:32; John 21:15-17). Wilson asserts that this formulation of unity in the individual "disciple community is true to the intention of the universal Church."[24] Before Jesus' ascension to Heaven, he gave authority to His disciples to pass on His teachings under the authority that He had been given by God. Accordingly, the disciples, as constituents of His assembly, were the first to be instructed by Jesus the Christ, in the good news and chosen to bear witness of this good news. Therefore, the disciples being a model for the first assembly of the elect in the New Testament Church recognized "the good news to which the Church has been called as fundamentally a way of life to be acted out and practiced" and that God has purposed that His covenant of Grace would encompass every believer.[25] Early church history suggests the original disciples performed variegated, differentiated and centralized roles in and outside of the church. It suggests that "Paul was not the only effective missionary" and "long before Christianity expanded throughout every province of the Roman Empire and outside to Mesopotamia; penetrating every social class, the apostles had disappeared."[26] Discipleship is a process without end during this mortal existence (I Cor. 13:12). Every believer as a member of the local church is a constituent of that particular congregation and recognizably under its direction both as an expression of the discipleship and training imparted; and for continued empowerment and preparation as emissaries of Christ. The journey of disciple making is depicted in Scripture as the development and dissemination of the early church.

In the Church Jesus is Triumphant

"Hear, O Israel! The LORD is our God, the LORD is one" (Deut. 6:4). The premise of this monotheistic statement of Judaism is that only one God exists for all mankind. This is an unconventional conception considering that all references to Judaism implicitly propose a religion centered on distinctions based on genealogy. Israel was to become "a light to the nations, a sacrificial lamb and an atoning victim for the sins of the world."[27] Old Testament biblical theology portray a people who have been identified as a nation with whom God the Creator of the universe endeavors to allow accessibility to Himself. Judaism, the religious system compiled in the Hebrew Scriptures of Ancient Israel conveys a struggle in God's plan for creation imposed by the will of mankind. The Old

Testament nation of Israel inherited laws as an embodiment of this perfect relationship. However, Israel's human condition incessantly disrupted God's plan to form an ecclesiastical kingdom. The entire biblical record attests to efforts at reconciliation with God. "In defining Judaism, sages maintained possession of the Torah revealed by God to Moses which was passed down by men of the great assembly.[28]

Meetings in synagogues enabled individuals to maintain relationship with God, attain knowledge about Him, encounter Him through prayer and in holy assemblies as teachers and disciples. Faith in one God formed the foundation of Judaism and the requisite relationship with God expressed as total love, commitment and obedience (Deut. 6:5). Every generation of the nation of Israel expected the coming of their Lord and God as a familiar representation of Old Testament Israel and He arrives as propitiation in the New Testament Church of Christians. Demonstrated restoration and continuity exists between Old Testament Israel and the New Testament Church. Christianity confronted multiple lines of demarcation in defining itself apart from Judaism. It was notably an expansion of a "redefined Israel" as noted by the discourse between Jesus and the Canaanite woman signifying the extension of the benefits of election for Israel beyond the normative realm of Judaism; and the elimination of boundaries demonstrated by the conversion of Cornelius of Caesarea, a Roman centurion, who through the teachings of Phillip called the Evangelist, was embraced as a member of the body of believers (Mark 7:24-30; Acts 10).[29] In the New Testament church, the Old Testament ecclesia sought to maintain consensus regarding worship as God required, insisting that everyone associated were responsible in the assembly (Acts 21:24-26). Followers of Jesus were to accept particular responsibility by virtue of propriety; "a single Son, and a single law, together mediating the same Spirit."[30] The amalgamation of peoples established through baptism in Jesus' name proliferated New Testament churches. A new perspective on the continuity between the Old Testament Israel and the New Testament Church was popularized predicated upon the conviction that God's spirit was available through Christ to those outside Israel as well as to those within.[31] Because Jesus is triumphant, the Church became the newly assembled community of the chosen and faithful people of this one true God. The peoples of this New Testament church identified themselves as a community of persons *called out* by God to respond positively to the gospel message of salvation, separating themselves from the control of Satan and sin in society; and gathered in more than one place in a village or town, having more than one building in which to assemble.

The word church has been given two applications in the community of Christians: the entire body of the chosen and redeemed throughout and including the present era and to a singular or local congregation of professed believers.[32] The local church was a means through which disciples achieved maturity. The term, church is used to refer to an assembly of people summoned for a purpose (Acts 7:38; 8:1). Laymon states that the church is "not simply and aggregation or association of individual parts, but an organic entity which is metaphysically as real as an individual's existence is real; it is an extension of the person of Christ."[33] Therefore, the primary definition of a local church is a visible, living, earthly corporation of believing Christians confirmed by growth, development, engaging in fellowship and acts of worship. According to *The American Heritage Dictionary of the English Language*, the word "church" is derived from a Greek word, *kuriakon (doma)* which means house of the Lord and was adopted by the Christian community as referencing the place where believers assemble acknowledging that these gatherings are of people who belong to the Lord.[34] Although found less commonly in the original language of the Bible, this Greek word has been used to mean houses of Christian worship since 300 A.D.[35] During the early centuries, all Christians expressed membership in a particular community through baptism which was a demonstration of their acceptance of the gospel message and representative of the chosen people of God.

According to the text, *The Early Church*, "Israel was already an ecclesia, a congregation of the faithful and elect people of God among whom were individuals set apart to carry out particular functions."[36] For the apostles and the Jewish community of Christians as a newly formed communal colony, it was simultaneously a new conception of religious fellowship and a continuation of the old membership. The inclusion of converted Gentiles and Christians corroborated the restoration and continuity between the Old Testament and the New Testament Church acknowledging one God for mankind. Still steeped in tradition, the church became a concentrated community with its usual concerns for its leaders, widows and helpless; "concerned with its own life and purity of doctrine, determined to be blameless before the nonbelievers, but utterly unconcerned with their affairs."[37] The church was the observable means through which Jesus was triumphant, where pilgrimage under the authority of one God and Lord was certain and was observed as a kingdom model where *the Truth* was lived without compromise.

Beyond the Apostolic Church

The church's inception during the Apostolic Era afforded the foundation for the responsibilities of this newly formed assembly. Unlike modern times, the socio-political agenda of the surrounding society did not have primacy; at issue were welcoming non-Jewish people into the church community of the elect, the necessity to become a Jew before embracing the faith and imposing Jewish practices and prohibitions on Gentiles (Acts 15). In the early centuries, the church meant a community of Christians (Acts 11:26). According to Comby, "the church which was first and foremost a local community formulated in various cities having a large measure of autonomy within their respective countries" constituted individuals with diverse cultural, political and economic backgrounds.[38] The Bible depicts the church as having the responsibility to provide spiritual leadership, discipleship training; and to address issues contrary to the maintenance of the Christian community. Dissimilar to contemporary perspectives the local church as an institution did not make those outside of the community the focus of its endeavors but encouraged discipleship to exemplify teachings to the unbelieving world.

Following Jesus' ascension, the early church comprised believers and inquirers of the Gospel who were taught by the apostles that Christ was the fulfillment of Judaism. Christian believers did not meet in buildings dedicated for worship but met in common places or individual homes. Each local church assembled separately across the country, but were universally connected illustrating the united faithful throughout the world. Demonstrably a contradictory movement from the established Jewish community the rationale for local meeting places afforded familial identification, spiritual growth and maturation. However, the church was often kept secret, fearing persecution. Each region, African, Asian, and Roman for example, had to contend with persecution as resentment grew even within the body of faithful for its acceptance and engagement in the various worldly influences based on religious treason, social and political precepts. Persecution of the church involved repossession of Scriptures which were deemed illegal and the prohibition of assembly which led to the burning of books and the demolition of churches. Historical literature contends that Christianity was vehemently in opposition to the perspectives and philosophical views of Greek and Roman rule. The curious who chose to be present during assembly may have been converted by the presence and power of God however, those reluctant to the Gospel remained separated and were not in attendance during Christian assembly. New believers were prompted by the Holy Spirit, established through communication of the Gospel message outside of the assembly and by the exhibition of the truths in Scripture directly in speeches or indirectly through deed. Considering the necessary concealment of the churches location, the process of conversion, though possibly carried out by the local church leadership, was most probably performed away from the church by laypersons individually or in groups. These efforts preceded the resultant titles of missionary or para-church.

Transformation of the church "emerged as social institutionalization of Christianity, first in the Jewish socio-historical context and then, in a Greco-Roman context."[39] The political forces surrounding the church influenced its activities and mission; inevitably, progressively more parallels were ascertained by theologians between the Roman Empire and the Christian church. Church history provides insights into the scholarly approaches and kinship authority utilized to address problems within the church effecting solutions which emerged as counsels and creeds. Various groups emerged alleging their authority as successors of apostolic leadership and conveying separate theological schools of thought. Textual analysis of early church history indicates that the many changes in the structure and practices of the church have been due to the determination of various successors, councils and individuals reporting the receipt of revelation. During the transition beyond the apostolic church, biblical assertions were exchanged for theological doctrine of the church which developed as "the existential relationships of humans to God, to one another in community and the created universe."[40] Early church history substantiates an ecclesia wrought with dissension, although, the biblical theme of the New Testament Church is unity of the community of faith expressed as hope and love in communion together with God. The transitory history of the church, according to Lawler, affirms that "the church and its structures are not ultimate, but only a means to communion."[40] The tumultuous history of the church attests that the irrefutable reality of the church is not due to "structure, doctrines, laws or sacraments" it exists because God has predestined it (Rom. 8:29-30).[42]

Chapter Summary

The New Testament Church met in various edifices which became the meeting place for worship, the Eucharist, fellowship and prayer; and notably to be called the local church. "The distinguishing feature as a member of the local body was baptism."[43] Scripture contends that the Church, local and universal, is to prepare all believers to be fit for specificity of service consistent with the will of God (Eph. 4: 11-13). Each member is required to become disciples of Christ and to develop others as disciples. Becoming like Christ is a lifelong experience, therefore each must rely on the Holy Spirit to fulfill His promised provision of the "fruits of patience, love, kindness, faithfulness, joy, peace, goodness, gentleness and self-control" (Gal. 5: 22-23). In the Bible, developed leaders and ministers of the Christian community dispersed gospel throughout the inhabited world. Some were assigned by the church such as Timothy; others were guided by the Holy Spirit through revelation, such as Paul (Acts 13:4; 16:3). The Bible declares that God loves humankind whom He created and does not desire that "any should perish, but come to repentance" (II Pet. 3:9). The onslaught of sin against a righteous Creator, demands justice; and justice demands a resolution which humanity is unable to pay. God provides a resolution through Grace, in the form of Jesus Christ our Savior, as a way for mankind to escape the consequences of aberrant behaviors. The Bible narrative provides the process by which God has presented opportunity for reinstitution of mankind to recover residency in the kingdom of God. "The theme of the kingdom; its founding, disruption and restoration" is the nucleus, beginning with the first book of the Old Testament to the last book of the New Testament; "all the other elements including the issues surrounding church formation, Christian leadership, evangelism and human subjection must find their places beneath this theme."[44]

The local church as the conception for the kingdom of God is significant in the exposition of the para-church-local church controversy. Biblical emphasis of the New Testament alleges that the sole responsibility of the church is to preach the kingdom of God and teach about the Lord, Jesus Christ. Each church was infused with the social and political influences of its surrounding cultures which distorted the original apostolic foundation and enacted various religious forms of government established by the reigning authority of the region. Scripturally and theologically the local church was ordained an assembly of the elect under the headship of Christ.

Each individual location is a place where an "alliance and congregation is formed as a body knit together by the sense of one belief, united in discipline, and bound together by a common hope."[45] The goal of the early church was common sanctity within an ecclesiastical framework. In every believer's heart and mind was the divine notion of a life controlled by and in existence for God. They regarded themselves as separate from the rest of the world, bound together by peculiar ties, finding solace within each geographically-located tabernacle and cooperation among the brethren when travel was eminent for disciple-making away from the local church. We are living in the twenty-first century of the early church. Within the biblical context of the local church as a communal colony and by definition of the para-church as those who minister outside of the local church, every believer is individually, collectively and simultaneously a member of the para-church. Is Christ divided? "Hear, O Israel! The LORD is our God, the LORD is one" and Scriptures pronounce that we are <u>one</u> in Him, affording the biblical foundation for cooperation between the church and the para-church (Deut. 6:4)

CHAPTER 2

THE SPIRITUAL INHERITANCE OF ALL
BELIEVERS

The Bible states that the believer "must be born again" to receive the spiritual inheritance; that believers having been born again are a recreated spirit in Christ and that Jesus' heritage belongs to anyone born of the Spirit (John 3:3; Gal. 2:20; 4:6-7). "Blessed be the God and Father ... who has caused us to be born again to a living hope... to obtain an inheritance which is imperishable and undefiled and will not fade away, reserved in heaven" (I Pet. 1: 3-4). A new life for the Christian begins the moment that individual believes the Gospel through an apparent supernatural confidence in the Lord Jesus Christ for salvation. At that moment, God provides each new believer with a great number of unique and permanent promises. These promises that comprise the inheritance for the believer are comprehensive unconcealed doctrinal promises upon which the Christian may depend. Consequently, each individual believer is given the authority of discipleship and priesthood with the commission to teach the gospel and disciple-making. Christians have the assurance of a spiritual inheritance by the Holy Spirit that the Father is faithful in keeping His promises (Heb. 10:23). According to W. E. Vine, "inheritance strictly means to receive by lot; to receive as one's own and to obtain."[1] The definition is expounded further in view of the New Testament promises "to include receipt of all spiritual good provided through and in Christ", such as birthright, the Holy Spirit and God's covenant of Grace which incorporates justification, redemption, deliverance, position and salvation.[2] An inheritance is only valid subsequent to death of the owner. In the case of believers, the acknowledgement of Jesus Christ, the Son of God, and acceptance of Christ's resurrection from His atoning death on the cross with repentance are the rudiment of a relationship with the Father. John 1:12 and 14 states "we beheld the glory of the only begotten from the Father; and as many as received Him, to them He gave the right to become children of God, even to those who believe on His name;" and later Scripture states that "for you are all sons of God through Jesus Christ *having* received a spirit of adoption as sons by which we cry out, Abba! Father!" (Gal. 3:26; Rom. 8:15). According to God's grace and mercy all believers receive His spiritual inheritance. The concept of the divine fatherhood of God in Jesus with its accompanying spiritual inheritance for every believer, forms the biblical basis for cooperation between the church and the para-church and it is affirmed by Oswald Chambers who writes: "by creation we are all children of God; we are not the sons and daughters of God by creation; Jesus Christ makes us sons and daughters of God by regeneration" (John 1:12).[3]

The apparent unity of the Father and son in relationship is an expressed bond of love between God, the Father and Jesus which is to be expressed by the church, the sons and daughters of God (John 13:38; I John 4:7). "Through Jesus, Christians are led into a new, intimate relationship with God as their heavenly Father. Jesus does not speak of God as the Father of all men, but only of His own;" only by the human perspective of anticipation does he speak of the "unregenerate as being potentially God's children."[4] The sacrifice of Christ as the atonement, despite the depravity of humanity is God's gift of love to mankind. Our Lord lived on earth in a physical body, and demonstrated discipleship in that Jesus came to do the Father's will. He exhorted His followers to be diligent in understanding His mission and empowered them to accept their positions as sons and daughters of God and disciples of Christ. God is not simply the Supreme Being, but God and Father. "One of the foremost elements in the relations between God and man," the conceptual perspective of fatherhood elicits the affect of love between God and humanity exhibited through the many biblically recorded offers of redemption (Heb. 12:9).[5] The contention of the entire Bible is that "God is love;" the ultimate relationship (I John 4:8, 16). This is understood from the beginnings in Genesis to the expectations in Revelation. God's availing personal presence and fervency towards mankind; His emphasis on forgiveness, mercy, healing, self-sacrifice, sustaining life for eternity, feeding the hungry and community can be attributed to a nature full of compassion and love. The sons and daughters of God, the church, are disciples of Christ who, being of the same Spirit like Christ, inherit distinct characteristics of God's nature.

The Bible states that all believers are "raised up and seated with Jesus Christ" establishing the certainty of divine inheritance in Him (Ep. 2:6). This spiritual inheritance of believers begins with the lordship of Jesus Christ. The revelation of adoption as children of God is given by inspiration of the Holy Spirit which is exercised in every believer (Gal. 4:6, 7). The spirit of adoption experienced by the believer is not primarily a reference to the transaction by which God has made believers His children, but to an awareness of the reality that as His children every believer can enter His presence without fear or hesitation having confidence in their relationship of true intimacy as an heir. Jesus prayed that the unity of love and purpose which "He has with the Father will be reflected by His disciples," God's adopted children; "and that the mission which Jesus received and fulfilled from His Father will be the same mission of all who find joy fulfilled in being His disciple throughout all times and ages" (John 17).[6] "Knowledge of God involves the capacity" of the church to ascertain the source of its existence, "hear and respond to God's call, and accept within its framework Christ's own loving disposition—His humility unto death."[7] The biblical perspective that every Christian, are God's adopted children, having the mind of Christ "to will and to do according to His good pleasure" supports cooperation between the church and the para-church (Phil. 2:2). Such purposive communion is attributable to the acknowledged spiritual inheritance of every believer manifested by the Holy Spirit, as each presents the conduct of a new life within the community and to the world.

THE STATE OF GRACE IS GIVEN TO ALL BELIEVERS

The rationale for the new life of a believer is the love of God in Jesus Christ and the spiritual inheritance is attributable to His grace. By His grace, the Church acquires all that encompasses the heritage of Christ as its spiritual inheritance such as relationship with the Father, the Holy Spirit as comforter and guide; power and authority, eternal life with the Father and the Son, membership in the family of God, even rejection and persecution. Blackaby states "sin has affected humanity so deeply," that it is impossible to pursue God on one's own volition; relationship must be initiated by

God (John 6:44-45, 65).[8] God's covenant of Grace is exemplified in His consignment of adoption. He has bestowed unmerited favor on every believer in the form of a gift which includes justification, redemption, deliverance, position and salvation. Justification "denotes the act of pronouncing acquittal from guilt; all that was necessary on God's part to establish the believer's righteousness has been effected in the death of Jesus Christ and facilitated in his resurrection and life. Redemption is another word for recovery or rescue and indicates that an intervening or substitute action has consummated liberation from an undesirable condition. It alleges a price as a requirement for release. "God alone provides atonement or expiation for sin through His son Jesus Christ by which His wrath is assuaged."[9] Deliverance depicts release; to change from or make free as granted by favor. It is demonstrated as the believer is translated from the power of death, through Jesus who "bringing many sons to glory, delivered those who through fear of death were subject to slavery all their lives," unto life everlasting (Heb. 2:10-15). Position connotes status. The believers' status is observed in God's covenant of Grace which proclaims adoption into God's eternal family; that Jesus "shared in flesh and blood, being made like His brethren in all things that he might become a merciful, high priest in things pertaining to God to make propitiation for the sins of the people" (Heb. 10: 14-17) "Salvation is the spiritual and eternal condition granted by God to those who accept His conditions of repentance and faith."[10]

The state of grace is given to all believers. Scripture presents the description of two human beings representative of the initiating covenant of Grace with God and humanity (I Cor. 15: 21-22). The first man God created, He named Adam, and established an eternal relationship with mankind. The second man, named Jesus is inferred as the second Adam and according to the New Testament of the Bible, all believers are adopted and made children of God by this second Adam (I Cor. 15: 45). Grace is an eschatological schema demonstrating God's predilection for relationship with humanity. Grace denotes the relational characteristics of God declaring that He is "not too remote to care" for the humankind He created.[11] The state of grace is given to all saints with its emphasis on privileged position in Christ leading to final deliverance. Grace is a corollary to God's creation of humanity and the axiom on which biblical truths are erected. Forgiveness is the divine miracle of grace along with the supernatural indwelling of the Spirit of God. Grace is manifested as the ability to enter into complete identification with Jesus Christ. Grace is God's divine response to the harsh reality of our need for salvation.

Grace asserts that once an individual, Jew or Gentile is admitted into the Church through Christ, "they become saints or holy, because they belong to the people of God and are worshipping Him as revealed in the Christian redemption."[12] Grace expresses that "God's oversight of the world is personal and universal, encompassing both the spiritual and material needs of people."[13] Grace is the spiritual inheritance of every Christian. Grace is in the Gospel of Jesus Christ; "the Gospel is the power of God for salvation to everyone who believes" and its proclamation is the task of every member of the church (Rom. 1:16; Mark 16:15).

Grace Discharges Law

Every believer receives as a spiritual inheritance the final covenant of Grace which entails a life characterized by love rather than laws, culminating in the attainment of an eternal union with God. It is love demonstrated as unselfish, unconditional, unmerited beneficence. The focus of the Law is primarily on the temporal, material and mundane aspects of Christianity which loses sight of the personal relational responsibility and action-based supernatural giftedness of the Holy Spirit. Jesus informed the masses that he came to fulfill the Mosaic Law that formed the basis for identifying sin. In the book of Galatians, the contention is that the law has the consequence to restrain sin but where there is love, no law is required (5: 22). To contrast the spiritual inheritance of Grace with mankind's implementation of the law: the law exploits while grace respects, the law isolates, grace embraces, the law divides, grace unifies, the law elicits pride while grace establishes humility; and the law reaps distinction, while grace sows likeness. There are many affirmations supporting the biblical perspective for cooperation between the church and the para-church as each acquiesce to the receipt of grace given each believer with established privileges and the ability to communicate with God, comprehend Scripture, and minister in the name of Jesus according to the sanctifying Spirit that enables believers to know what is the perfect will of God (Rom. 12:2; I Cor. 2:16). Despite sufferings and persecutions by many who abided under the Mosaic Law and those with a secular resolve, Paul pronounced that "God's grace is sufficient" (II Cor. 12:9). Through the covenant of Grace, Jesus' sacrifice on the cross eliminated the necessity for human mediation, established the unifying identity for the entire body of believers, purposed through the church edification of the body, furtherance of His kingdom and the universal bond of Christianity.

Grace Manifests Relationship

With grace comes familial relationship in Christ. Jesus became intercessor and the allowance of direct communion with the Father was endowed through Him (Heb. 4:14-16; I Tim. 2:5). The various names and identifiers listed in Scripture for the children of God emphasizes the different aspects of the believer's relationship with Him, notably Christian, saint, brethren, sons, daughters, bride, branches, elect, chosen, servant and royal priesthood. Note that all terms are corporate and interrelated; re-emphasizing a community of familiar people. The receipt of the Holy Spirit accompanies a new relationship with God. Paul calls this new relationship adoption (Rom.8:15). There is a familial relationship without minimizing the deity and oneness of God. The concept of familial relationship presupposes that God being the Creator and Father of all men established mankind as His children (John 1:12-13). The believer is transferred into a new existence by this renewing Spirit of God, leaving one's natural family and entering into the privileges and responsibilities of the spiritual family (I Cor. 6:14-18). Being sons and daughters with Christ the believers' acceptance is not unjust or arbitrary (Rom. 9:14-15).[14] The familial relationship with God, our Spiritual Father and every believer is preordained. All believers are disposed to call God "Father;" all receive the Holy Spirit, spiritual gifts, are disciples and all believers are granted the benefit of being heirs with authority, rights and privileges (Rom. 8:15; Gal. 4:5-7). As members of God's holy family, Scripture establishes the church as an "enduring entity formed by appeal to common origin which is supernatural, produced by God's command, uniform, united, not meant to suffer discrimination or diminished status, and subject to God's love and concern" (Eph. 1:4-10).[15] The whole family is enabled and required to manifest the mysteries of the gospel for the maturation of believers and the unbelieving world as the universal Church which constitutes the local church and para-church (I Cor. 4:1; Eph. 6:19). The Bible narrates transcendent matters pertaining to a relationship between God and humanity, without distinction, and the formulation of a representative adopted family who are adapted for His eternal purpose to encompass a relatively opposing society (Amos 3:2; Rom. 9:23-26).

Grace Empowers Destiny

There are present and future components of the spiritual inheritance. The present reality of the believer's adoption into the family of God is release from the bondage of sin and the Mosaic Law, imputed righteousness through Jesus Christ sealed with the Holy Spirit and a new position in Christ after faith and repentance to be free heirs of God. The future aspect of spiritual inheritance is salvation unto an eternal destiny with Him. Christians wait expectantly for the redemption of our bodies and freedom from the present corrupt world (Rom. 8:23). Adopted children of God have the advantage of becoming like Christ and being conformed to a glorious, immortal body (I John 3:2; Phil. 2:21). Salvation which is every believer's spiritual inheritance has no contingency based on status, position, geography or demography. It is based on union with Christ and the divine life in the Spirit which flows from this union to accomplish God's purpose. Since spiritual inheritance has death as its contingency familial relationship as the Divine Covenant of Grace "is seen through the window of incarnation and sacrifice."[16]

"The Lord Jesus at a particular time in the past became that which He was not before; a physical being; prior to that He was essentially as Spirit" (John 4:24).[17] The creation story informs of humankind's development to become a living presence; males and females uniquely made in the image of God (Gen. 2:27). God breathed into man and he became a living being. The breath of life symbolizes introduction of the spirit. The complexity of humanity comprising mind, body and spirit pervades the New Testament and provides representation of the nature of mankind. From the beginning God's Covenant of Grace preserved humanity. Every believer resembles God in the aspect of having an immortal spirit. Scripture attests that the human spirit has an affinity with God and that His spiritual reality operates on human consciousness (Acts 17: 23-24, 28-29). "As the Spirit" who descended upon Jesus following His baptism "is God's Spirit, so the Spirit who indwells Christians is God's Spirit;" and it is this same Spirit "who raises every believer to a new quality of life in fellowship of the Triune God:" the Father, Son and Holy Spirit, "whom we now call *Father*" (Rom 8:14-17).[18] The spiritual inheritance of all believers is having been made anew in Christ Jesus. The New Testament teaches that "the regenerated person, through the recreating work of the Holy Spirit and has communion with God as spirit with spirit. Jesus Christ comes as the Spirit-bearing man who promises the Spirit to His followers who are permanently transformed, Spirit-endued persons."[19] This community of Spirit-endued persons has been established to represent as Christ's existing spiritual earthly body legitimized by the centrality of Christ (I Cor. 12:27; Eph. 1:22; 3:10). By God's grace, "the same Spirit that anointed Jesus and enabled Him to fulfill God's divine plan, now also anoints every follower of Jesus" toward their individual divine destiny.[20]

Grace Characterizes the Church

Every believer represents a local church internally and externally. The Church, confidently expecting the final reward of a "new heaven and earth" which is both spiritual and visible, is to be the full expression of the covenantal relationship of grace in Christ who was a teacher, exhorter and lover of humanity with a heart of acceptance, compassion, forgiveness and love (Rev. 21:1). Grace characterizes the church. The uniqueness of grace expressed in Scripture evokes the persistent exposition that a ubiquitous, absolute and sovereign God would initiate pardon for the inconsistencies of humanity. An all-sufficient Creator devised a plan whereby mankind, made in His image could be restored communally and as His church administer the revelation of restitution to the lost. The Word of God says that when Jesus, the teacher and basis of the New Testament church departed, the Holy Spirit, the pledge of mankind's spiritual inheritance, was presented as a guide for the church (John 14:16, 26; 16: 13). The Church as a body "functions through the faithful use of its member's various gifts and sovereignty uniquely bestowed by the Holy Spirit."[21] God finds no deficiency in Jesus through whom each believer is presented as acceptable (Rom. 3: 21-24). Chambers states that "the marvelous thing about the spiritual inheritance is when we take our part of it everyone else is blessed in the taking; but if we refuse to be partakers of the inheritance *or disable the elect* we rob others of its glory and wonder."[22] Grace characterizes the church. All believers, serving God in the local church and the para-church, are equal before the Lord, for because of His grace and by His Spirit all are His children, current and future citizens of His eternal kingdom, recipients of His spiritual inheritance, and sanctified commissioned for His purpose.

Grace Authorizes Position

Grace authorizes position in Christ. "The Spirit consecrates the elect so that they are possessed and controlled by God, rendering their due obedience of faith to Jesus Christ."[23] All believers in Jesus Christ as Messiah have the position of justification without inadequacy. Justification is a legal or forensic term meaning righteous or pardoned from guilt and penalty. The designation of this position means that Christ's righteousness is imputed to the believer's account enabling God's acceptance. Representation of the believer's position is demonstrated within the spirit-filled body called the universal Church; and the nature of the local church is suggested in the metaphor of a "spiritual house constructed of living stones…a chosen people, royal priesthood, a race and nation" (I Pet. 2:5-9). Each member of the local church having entered into relationship with the triune God is equally endowed with the miraculously given Spirit of God's divine nature to display the image and proclivity of His Son, Jesus Christ; each is justified, presented as His children and citizens of His eternal kingdom (Eph. 1:3-13). According to the text, "in the Old Testament era, the Holy Spirit was given primarily to people who occupied official positions in the theocracy of Israel such as kings, priests, judges and prophets."[24] These positions were assigned according to tradition, birthright or subjugation. The position of justification "for the Christian in the New Israel is due to the call of God" (I Pet. 2:9).[25] The New Covenant of grace revisits the mission of the Holy Spirit as resting on all of God's people and not solely on "official leaders."[26] This was evident by the outpouring of the Spirit at Pentecost on the assembly of those speaking and hearing the Word of God who selected repentance and gained salvation. Much like the religious sects in Jesus' day, the determination of religious leadership predicated upon genealogy, monarchy, lot and succession often suggests a selective process that designates certain individuals for roles and responsibilities based on human affectation. These appear to be apart from the sanctifying work of the Holy Spirit inevitably ensuring the development of Christian pietism which is disconnected from Christian practice. As a portion of spiritual inheritance the Holy Spirit gives life to the believer. Without the receipt of the Holy Spirit and rebirth mankind does not have an intrinsic relationship in Jesus and expressions of belief are religious aspects of tradition and ritualism (John 3:3, 6). Tradition and ritualism can become familiar whereby adherents fastidiously observe the details while neglecting its heart.[27] The Scriptures affirm that the inclination is that demonstrations of tradition and rituals afford special rights and privileges (Mat. 3:7-9; 23:6, 7). This is theoretically represented by the older brother in the narrative of the prodigal son who avowing of his own goodness, demonstrating adherence to tradition and ritual; and begrudging the younger brother their father's attentions demonstrates contempt and an air of entitlement, much like the church-para church relationship, which can manifest as being relentless in judgment of spiritual things leading to encumbrances (Luke 15: 28-30; I Cor. 2:10). Jesus warned the religious leaders of His day that haughtiness and despotism are examples of estrangement from God and consequently, those who exalt themselves and their own ideals above the desires of God receive a fitting inheritance (Mat. 6:1, 2, 5; Luke 16:15).

The New Testament presents a covenant of inclusion for all believers; for the expansive work of the Kingdom (Mat. 9:37; Luke 10:2). Jesus admonished believers to conduct themselves as a community having compassion and love; and not to disengage from profiting each other (I Cor. 10:33; 12:7). In order to implement the divine purpose of God, each believer, being justified through faith is given instruction which requires obedience. Hebrews, chapter 11, reminds us of the triumphant faith and obedience to God revealed by outstanding believers, who preceded the New Testament Church. The faith of the saints and martyrs of old demonstrate that each individual being justified is designed and appointed to perform their duty and may receive assignment by God apart from the local assembly. Guided by faith their loyalty to God enabled them to destroy pagan cities, subdue kingdoms, close the mouths of lions, quench the hostility of fire, escape the edge of the sword, wax valiant in battle, and turn to flight the armies of foreign invaders (Heb. 11:33-34). Affirming their justification, by grace New Testament believers "chose to endure ill-treatment, esteemed the reproach of Christ greater riches than earthly treasures," forsook pagan cultures, obeyed God despite heritage and tradition; and in the Lord's strength through faith, attempted the impossible, performed miracles and obtained promises (Heb. 11: 25-34). Some were persecuted, jailed or martyred for what they believed (Heb. 11:35-37). Scripture affirms that all of God's children through faith and repentance are justified by God's grace to receive an equal right to His spiritual inheritance. The Bible instructs its readers that Christians have position in Christ, through the Holy Spirit and all are accountable to the Father. Christians are to be light in the world (Mat. 5: 14-16). Analogous to Jesus and the saints of old, every Christian is required to fulfill God's calling to witness to others about the Lord Jesus Christ and to receive the promised reward (Matt. 28:19; John 20:21; Acts 10:42).

Grace Affords Privilege

To elucidate the grandeur of the spiritual inheritance afforded believers, the Bible asserts that every Christian has the privilege of a royal priesthood. The relational aspect of the royal priesthood in God's earthly purpose is significant to the universal Church. The expression *royal priesthood* infers that the members are the priests of a king. It is a designation of honor as one being called of God, ordained to serve by the offering of gifts and sacrifices on behalf of men in things pertaining to the Almighty King; "priests were set apart to serve the Lord and to minister to Him in worship" (Heb. 5:1, 4).[28] As priests, believers are assigned a reputable status, being selected by God as His "special people chosen for the purpose to proclaim the praises of Him who called us out of darkness into light, being zealous for good works and sharing the good news" (I Pet. 2:9). The Old Testament describes membership of the priesthood as an elite office with responsibilities of service, burden-bearer and witness (Num. 18:1-7). Historically, the priesthood had been a matter of birthright and the office was held for life. The elect were to be free of defilement, as symbolized by being ceremonially cleansed. Christ has imputed His righteousness on every believer that this New Testament generation of priests may be free of defilement before the Lord (Rom. 5). The royal priesthood of believers denotes a community with specific office, rank, quality and ministry. The Church as the royal priesthood is a body of priests, with the directive of "showing forth the Lord's excellence."[29] Notwithstanding, the need for order and organization necessitates the institution of specific leadership in the church, "the New Testament does not acknowledge a sacerdotal class in contrast to laity; all believers whether Jew or Gentile are constituted a kingdom of priests" and are commanded to obedience and sacrifice (Rev. 1:6; Rom 12:1-2).[30] The privilege of priesthood affords concessions which include an influential membership status in the family, distinct social standing, advantage of presentation before Jesus, the High Priest, notable rights, responsibilities and mercies. "As Jesus is the Messiah, King of the New Kingdom, his subjects are a priesthood continuing the role of Israel as the priestly people" (Ex. 19:6; Deut. 7:6; Gal. 6:16).[31] God has given every believer a measure of faith, diversity in gifting and election, with instruction that He appoints individuals into His service to declare the name of the Lord in all the earth (Rom. 12:3, 6; Ex 9:16). The priesthood of every believer, removes the Old Testament distinction between laity and clergy exacting the license and responsibility of all children of God to "draw near with confidence to the throne of grace;" to learn obedience experientially, as Jesus has done, and to always be subject to the will of the Father, the King, as heirs to the spiritual inheritance (Heb. 4:16; 5:8).

THE GREAT COMMISSION IS GIVEN TO ALL SAINTS

Jesus informed His disciples that a helper would be sent from the Father to bear witness of Him and that the disciples were to bear witness to the unsaved as those having received the Spirit of Truth (John 15:25-26; Acts 3:32). The Great Commission is noted in Scripture as the epitome of Christian service. According to Scripture believers will do "greater things" than Jesus who performed miracles, preached to produce conversion; and developed, instructed and expanded the Church (John 14:12). The proposed inception of the church is slated to be at Pentecost. The Pentecostal experience offers the assurance of unity in accordance to God's grace and the expression of community relative to conversion. During the Feast of Weeks which celebrated the conclusion of harvest on the fiftieth day, when the multitude of disciples gathered in their usual manner as a community of believers there was a manifestation of God's Holy Spirit. The resultant dialects spoken and heard by the individuals present was the distinctive manner by which Jesus was glorified and His commission advanced, as the participants in the assembly were informed of the gospel through the Holy Spirit. Following the witness and acceptance of Jesus Christ as Lord, the disciples unreservedly performed varied acts for evangelism. The quality of Jesus' ministry was matched by their enthusiasm as the Holy Spirit enabled these new disciples to act according to God's Great Commission to secure lost souls (Acts 2:41; 4:4). All Christians as saints of God have at their disposal the capacities of the Triune God to proclaim the Good News and to make disciples who are adherents of the faith.

A saint is a believer; an individual who is counted among the redeemed of the Lord and member of the Church. Under the influence of the Holy Spirit, the mission of the Church is to announce the justice and joy heralded by the Kingdom of God. To fulfill this mission the members of the body of Christ are given spiritual gifts which enable diverse forms of witness, service and office (I Cor. 12). God implores all of humanity to receive the good news of the Gospel and to accept their call to be God's people. It is Jesus' ministry of loving, liberating, reconciling, healing and serving which defines and shapes all ministries in His Church and the representative local church. The essential assignment of Christ is entrusted to all the people of God to execute endeavors of evangelism and discipleship to every nation. Through baptism all members commit to a local church, becoming part of the universal covenant community and are commissioned for service by the Holy Spirit. In this communal colony, the Holy Spirit unites those who follow Jesus Christ, assembles the local church; and assigns and sends saints as witnesses into a vast world.

Historically, society and the church developed a relationship of co-existence and people became "a part of a large community held together by their Christian faith."[32] The history of the early church depicts an era called the Patristic Period in which Christian leaders identified as *fathers* but recognized as priests, deacons, bishops, and teachers of the church; "preached sermons, prepared candidates for baptism, expounded on the Scriptures and encouraged Christians in the different stations of life."[33] John Chrysostom, noted as "the most prolific of the Greek *fathers*," wrote in his *Twentieth Homily on Acts* that "every Christian must be concerned for the salvation of his brothers; nothing is more frigid than a Christian who does not care for the salvation of others."[34] He provides various incidences in Scripture to confirm this position insisting that neither financial or class status, education or health has predominance in missions and ministry. He asserts that "nourished by Christ, everyone can profit his nature if he will fulfill his part."[35] The responsibility of the church through its membership is "the reconciliation of all individuals to God through Christ, who has made peace through the blood of His cross" (Col. 1:20; Eph. 1:9-10).[36] The Great commission, the spiritual inheritance of all who believe, is representative of biblical support for cooperation between the church and the para-church.

Power through the Holy Spirit

All saints have been given power through the Holy Spirit of God as a spiritual inheritance. A purpose of the gifting of the Holy Spirit is to provide comfort and security in a hostile world and to provide insight on how to enlighten the hearts and minds of mankind regarding their sinful condition and the realities of Christ. Jesus, presented as the High Priest who interceded for the lost, extended His ministry of intercession by imparting the ability to heal, cast out demons and perform miracles to His disciples (Mat. 10:7-8; Luke 10:17; Acts 4:16). He gave "authority over unclean spirits as evidence that the power of Satan was broken."[37] The coming of the Holy Spirit at Pentecost ushered in the empowerment of the saints in God's commission, compensated for the loss of Jesus' personal presence and instituted the Church. Jesus explained to Nicodemus that individuals born of the Holy Spirit are governed by the Holy Spirit which has the freedom like the wind. It cannot be observed, controlled or understood by human sensibilities but its effects are witnessed (John 3:8). "In the synoptic Gospels the Holy Spirit pervades the life, teaching and works of Jesus Christ, so it is for believers led by the Spirit."[38] The Holy Spirit is essential for mankind to live according to the intent of the gospel as its purpose is to guide in all truth. The outpouring of the Holy Spirit is the precursor for the future spiritual inheritance of believers ending with the emergence of a new order where God's kingdom reigns in the world. By the power of the Holy Spirit, the entire community of faithful has been "inaugurated into an era of new life made manifest in Jesus, who through His example gives an impulse to follow and the assurance, through His resurrection, that His followers will share in the supernatural work of their heroic deliverer."[39] As noted by Blackman, "it is simply that the Christian having learned through Christ what God is like in His concern for man's lack of righteousness, is open to receive God's gift of righteousness and from then on is under God's control" and powered by the Holy Spirit for His commission.[40]

Liberation and Love through Christ

With the receipt of the Father's love through the sacrifice of His Son, Jesus Christ sanctions the authority of the saints who have been commanded toward kingdom building. Authority refers to a relative position that an individual believer acquires through the Holy Spirit, with attendant rights, duties, lifestyle, honor and prestige in the body of Christ. Each saint, as a member of this elite, realizes their ultimate authority as a child of God receiving His spiritual inheritance with its requisite love through service. The Bible emphasizes that all believers are saved by the grace of God and not to be encumbered by the Law of Moses for in its place we have been offered the Law of Love, redeemed and made holy through Jesus Christ. Additionally, each believer, no longer under the requirements of the law but of love, has the manifestation of the Holy Spirit, is justified and in receipt of an established liberty; for Scripture states that "where the Spirit is, there is freedom" (II Cor. 3:17). "Liberation, wrought by the Spirit is God's gracious gift."[41] Spiritual liberation is characterized by the rendering of direct access from the God of love and the universal body of believers, the Church, exhibiting love for one another in opposition of the sinful nature (John 15:17).[42]

Love is to be demonstrated through ministration in the church and society. Within the community of the people of God there is, and has been since the early church, representative ministers called by God and set apart in the Church for distinguishable functions. A minister is defined and to be recognized literally and scripturally as a servant. Additionally, Vine's description of minister is decidedly based on the intended perspective, for example: "a servant in relation to his work, his master, his superior or public service."[43] Ministers are individuals who are Holy Spirit enlightened, gifted and assigned ministries; some to a position of leadership in the Church (I Cor. 12:4-11, 28-30). Ministries are given for the common good of the universal Church community to facilitate the efficacious dissemination of the gospel. Through gifts of communicating the gospel in word and deed, gifts of healing, caring, praying, teaching, giving, working for peace and justice every baptized believer is called to witness of Christ, to express in their daily lives the lordship of Christ and discipleship.

> For the Word of God is living and active, sharper than any two-edged sword, piercing to the division of soul and of spirit, of joints and of marrow, and discerning the thoughts and intentions of the heart. And no creature is hidden from His sight, but all are naked and exposed to the eyes of Him to whom we must give an account. (Heb. 4:12-13)

The Bible attests that the ministries of all members of the believing community are complementary, presenting as the biblical perspective which supports cooperation between the church and the para-church as saints are specified by grace, love and liberation through Christ.

Chapter Summary

Spiritual inheritance is not something earned or accumulated through self-effort, it is extended from the bounty of a generous benefactor and He has established that every Christian is mutually interdependent as His Church. Maintaining a conscience that is directed towards God as He is revealed in Jesus Christ, the church will find that it is brought to oneness with God and each other; for the assertion of Scripture is: "If we walk in the light, as He is in the light, we have fellowship one with another" and He that sanctifies and they that are sanctified are all one (I John 1:7; 17:20-21; Heb. 10: 10). Spiritual inheritance includes a finished and complete salvation *for all who believe* inseparably connected through faith and repentance. The New Testament contends that every believer has been redeemed because of the love of God; justified, and given power and authority by the righteousness of Jesus. Jesus is the "Savior and King" who "reconstitutes the people of God" as a royal priesthood.[44]

Every believer should be growing toward maturity in Christ and should be using their spiritual giftedness toward the completion of the Great Commission (Eph. 4:13-16). Every believer's life on earth is an antecedent to a future life where the darkness that currently resides will no longer exist. The covenant of grace makes this promise, as such; the Word of God is a manual defining parameters of this sojourn and the manner with which the children of God should behave toward one another. Scripture requires that a believer be identified as different, unique and uncommon exhibited by Christian fellowship and love being "members of one another" (Eph. 4:24). The Bible provides insight into the spiritual inheritance and its requisite commands to be imitators of Jesus; not allowing the cares, deceits and disruptive concepts of this world to invade God's doctrinal message. Scripture warns against false teachings and doctrinal communication that promotes position in Christ as "relative status which becomes a major determinant of the behaviors" children of God display "toward one another," and where "competition for this status becomes the prime motivator" (John 11:47).[45] As we consider the church-para-church controversy, these perspectives must be realized; as the Word says, "all things become visible when they are exposed by the light" (Eph. 5:13). The light is not evil, divisive, or foolish. It proclaims that all children of God receive the spiritual inheritance and are to be motivated by ONE Spirit from the SAME Lord to ONE purpose. Through sanctification, each member has been justified; "having no spot and no condemnation" (Rom. 8:1; Eph. 5:27). No one is the greater in the family of God, each believer has been liberated to love and service; all are mutually interdependent and equal.

The Bible states that "the Church is the body of Christ," subsequently the para-church-church controversy presents as "one hating its own flesh" (Eph. 5:29). Scripture affords the image of God, the Father presenting His son Jesus as a protector, loyal friend and savior who nourishes and cherishes His fellow heirs. The Bible affirms support for cooperation between the church and the para-church contending that every believer is an heir and disciple of Christ; required to be subject to God and each other. Emphasizing the believer's spiritual inheritance as a covenant between

God and humanity formulating the Church, is the account of marriage analogized in Scripture. The marriage analogy affirms that, individual members and emphatically those individuals assigned roles of leadership, are to nourish and cherish one another; "esteeming others as greater than themselves, knowing that there is only one Master of all; and there is no partiality with Him" (Acts 20:28; Eph. 6:9; Phil. 2:3).

CHAPTER 3

THE EMERGENCE OF THE PARA-CHURCH

Emerging from the matrix of Judaism, as the second identified monotheistic theology, Christianity has been beset with the encumbrances of other religious beliefs, practices, cultural movements and academia. The Protestant Reformation and modernity embraced the concept of multiple ecclesiologies which formed the basis of humanity's need to focus on a "central point of religious thought."[1] Characterized by the missional and improvisational perspectives of Christianity, the para-church developed "based on a philosophy to be evoked, governed and judged by the gospel" and whatever its tradition or organizational focus, "its activities and actions are determined and responsible to the good news of Jesus Christ" advocated by the church.[2] The para-church defined as a cooperative of faith-guided individuals emerged to heed the missiological ecclesiology of the church demonstrated as a "commitment to mission and concomitant flexibility while remaining faithful to God's commission."[3] Mission is herein defined as the worldwide enterprise of making disciples of nations outside the accessible and normative outreach of the local church. The church, performing its duty as assigned in Christ: teaches, trains and assists the development of spiritual maturity and leadership enabling disciples to continue the work of the Master in evangelizing the human race. These evangelizing efforts which became known as para-church organizations essentially assumed the initiation of activities to address the underrepresented concerns of Christians along with the unmet needs of the un-churched.

The concept of one God despite dogmatic differences is proposed in Christ as the foundation of the church and encompassed in the para-church which admonishes the biblical principle of unity through its practice of ecumenicalism. The biblical principle of unity introduces an edict which supports cooperation between the church and the para-church. Christians are exhorted to be one in Christ and to love one another as a witness to the world (John 17; Phil. 2: 1-16). This unity is inclusive of cooperation advocating a sense of shared spirituality. Following the creation of man and woman, the God of relationship brings the two together in a consummate marriage of "one flesh" (Gen. 2:23-24). This initial union may be regarded as the first identified type of church, depicting a required order, loyalty, communion and reciprocal responsibility (I Cor. 11:8-9.11-12). The concept of *one flesh* characterizes the *one God, one body, one spirit, and one baptism* distinguished in Scripture. In the marriage analogy, the husband is regarded as the head or leader in the marriage relationship as Christ is the head of the Church. The wife, or helper in Genesis, is analogous of the obedient, reverential Church, the universal assembly inclusive of its leadership, which is to receive love, protection, teaching, care and instruction from Christ through the husband, the local church (Gen. 2:18). Forsaking all others, the Church, "in whom His own life is completely identified," is to be contained only under the authority of Jesus (Eph. 5: 23, 25, 28-29, 33).[4] The para-church emerges as a component of this analogous marital relationship. Unity is additionally emphasized in God's invitation to discipleship and the adoption of "Jews, Gentiles, slaves and freemen" (I Cor. 12:13). Christian unity is promoted in Ephesians chapter four as sharing the Spiritual life within one body, the universal Church, though distinguished geographically. Scripture states that all believers are sealed and indwelt by the same Spirit; governed by one Lord and one system of fundamental truth, having one essential purpose and interdependence (Eph.1:18; 4: 4-11).Every member in the body is given a particular capacity for ministry through the impartation of spiritual gifts to effect spiritual benefit (Eph. 4:8). Missions, para-church organizations and other Christ-centered, charitable volunteer societies developed as the evidential product of unity in ministry. As the saints are equipped by the various spiritual leaders given to the Church, "to build up the body," these believers are to carry out the work of ministry through the use of the gifts of giving, administration, helps, teaching, evangelism, mercy, exhortation, prophecy and service; "until we attain the unity of the faith and of the knowledge of the Son of God, to a mature man, to the measure of the stature of the fullness of Christ" (I Cor.12; Eph. 4: 13). Scripture provides adequate confirmation of the universality of the local church and its mission to send laborers, disciples and workmen (Mat. 9:37-38; 28:19; II Tim. 2:15). Throughout each book there is evidence of God's unfailing love and limitless utilization of diverse resources to attain His purpose of reconciling fallen humanity to familial status (Eph. 3:15). Efforts that encompass this goal encourages unity; and is established and commissioned by God according to the purposes of God (Luke 10:1-2, 9; Acts 13:2-4; Gal. 1:15-17; Col. 1:25-27). The para-church is a vehicle which encourages Christians to work collaboratively outside and across denominational demarcations to accomplish this end. "Para-church organizations as a rule endorse the local churches and denominations in which their members fellowship."[5] As a derivation of the local church, para-church organizations engage the Church and the world.

Based on various perspectives and ascribed traits, difficulty is encountered in an effort to effectively describe what constitutes a para-church. Para-church does not mean a different church or separated from the church. Para is derived from the Greek language and by definition is a prefix signifying alongside of, beside, beyond and similar to. By extension from these senses, this prefix came to designate objects or activities auxiliary to or derivative of that which is denoted by the base word; and as an English prefix, para means ancillary or subsidiary, to identify roles requiring more training or of a higher status. Descriptors for the para-church comprise verbiage such as independent of the church, coming alongside the church for the purpose of assisting the church to accomplish its mission; and an unofficial organization of persons who are recognized as Christians in doctrine and practice. Many individuals within para-church organizations or groups have an established relationship in a local communal colony of the faithful and are often professionally or theologically trained. Having the perception of being members of the body of Christ through Spirit-given faith and repentance, these persons who may be constituents from various congregations and diverse backgrounds unite predicated upon the call of God and His invitation to the *marriage feast*, addressing a myriad of conditions for the churched and the un-churched to advance the purposes of God (Mat. 22:1-14; Rev.22:17).

INITIATED TO ADDRESS UNDERREPRESENTED CONCERNS

Many texts indicate that the emergence of the para-church organization was during the nineteenth century. Some cite that the original demonstrations were afforded the "Pietists in 1669."[6] Pietists promoted the "study of the Bible by laymen," which was unheard of and established a training center that "extended a new missionary movement to the world and expanded Christianity through laity and clergy"[7] Instead of reliance on a specific local church, these groups "devoted to the propagation of the faith" made appeals to a wide array of donors "and the burden for the enterprise was assumed by the growing number of newly instituted congregations."[8] With the conviction that the biblically sanctioned priesthood of all Christians includes laity they shared with clergy the responsibility to disseminate the gospel message."[9] This organized body of clergy and laity have been defined as the para-church considering their efforts were instituted and functioned outside of the authority of any specified local church. Scholars have noted the biblical account of several disciples including the Apostle Paul who were dispatched according to the Spirit of God to various cities as "New Testament missionaries;" functioning much like the para-church being under no specified local church authority.[10] Referencing his constitution in view of the para-church ideology, theologically, Paul's contention was "to become all things to all men, that I may by all means save some" (I Cor. 9:19-23). In an effort to save souls for Christ, Paul aspired to meet underrepresented concerns; to address the matters of people. Historically, the para-church has existed as an enterprise for many years, occasionally "referred to as social ministries, special purpose groups, voluntary societies, faith-based nonprofits and specialized institutional ministries."[11] Initiated as a mission of the New Testament church, similar to Paul's missionary journeys, these groups which are guided by the principles of the Word of God for disciple-making establish relations, minister to needs and engage in evangelism outside the confines of the local church edifice.

The "Para-church organization has both religiously-motivated and social objectives."[12] It has developed as a means of removing boundaries and barriers for evangelistic outreach to many geographic areas, cultures and countries. The para-church asserts itself as a component, as is every local church, of the universal Church having a common faith and the collective mandate of obedience to God in His purpose to reach out to the whole world which is outside of the edifice of the church. The proliferation of the para-church may be observed in many other aspects characteristic of discarding the church edifice as church members participated in taking the gospel to the people without the restrictions of denominationalism or association evidenced by the implementation of tent revivals, evangelistic crusades, discipleship ministries, mass communication ministries, and social activist groups. The formation of para-church organizations with its ecumenical, interdenominational character gained prominence with most needs-based societal groups, women and lay persons who were often underrepresented within the local church.[13] Interestingly, the occurrence of "Sunday School began as a para-church movement."[14] The beginning of the para-church as a method and ministry to disseminate the message of the gospel does not have exact delineations. However, the efforts of the para-church in building networks of independent entities address spiritual growth, moral maturity and societal change and its emergence is an acknowledgement that the call of God is to restoration of the lost and sanctifying those who have been restored.

Ministry of Edification through the Para-church

Scripture teaches that every believer is in the ministry. Ministry entails knowledge of what God requires of an individual believer and the major characteristic of ministry involves service. Jesus urged the disciples to be in service to one another and to service those outside of the faith by His Great Commission. Service to one another or "the equipping of the saints for the work of service, to the building up of the body of Christ," is illustrated in Christian literature and identified in the earliest philosophical teachings of scholars and the church councils that emerged centuries ago which sought to address underrepresented concerns (Eph. 4:12). To further exemplify the inception of para-church ideology, the Holy Bible, acknowledged as the inerrant Word of God, originally written in Aramaic, Hebrew and Greek has been translated by scholars, scribes and preachers in collaboration, many functioning independent of a local church, *to equip the saints* according to the ruling culture, customs and prevailing languages. Often formulated by philosophical treatise, political tensions and theologian reflection, supplemental materials were accepted by the church. As early as the Patristic Period between 100 b. c. and 451 b. c., there were "distinctive styles of theology associated with Platonic traditions that established the presentation of "patristic literature which augmented the Scriptures."[15] Study of Scripture "spans thousands of years evidenced as the interpretive writings of Sacred Hebrew Scriptures by Scribes and Priests, the church

43

fathers teaching and preaching and their exegetical heirs giving meaning and substantive influence to the Holy Word."[16] Commentaries were developed as theological luminaries instituted and became constituents of theological debate. Key cultural periods, spiritual themes and human individualism have been instrumental in the evolutionary process of the use of adjunctive media to expand Christian theology. Throughout the many historical periods: the Middle Ages, Renaissance, the Reformation to Modernity, the Holy Bible has been expanded upon by laity and clergy with the incorporation of media methods, the most prevalent being verbal, pictorial and written; some with the purpose to disseminate concepts which underlie or advance the discipline of Christian Theology, others to engage believers in the essentials of Christianity; all are inclusive activities of service performed by Christians ostensibly labeled the para-church.

Characteristically, the service performed by the para-church has different facets and manifestations such as the formation of Bible study groups, emergency aid centers, food pantries, disaster relief, student and youth outreach and domestic violence programs; but the common element dependent upon the nature of the ministry is the evidential spiritual profitability of the individual benefactor and beneficiary. According to the Scriptures, all believers must be restored, developed and fixed toward the common goal of being like Christ "for even the Son of Man did not come to be served, but to serve, and to give His life a ransom for many" (Mark 10:45; Eph. 4:12-13). The word *para-church* is a contemporary concept not found in Scripture, but their actions and efforts are a direct approach to God's specific command to teach, preach and make disciples of God's children who remain outside of the church as evidenced in the New Testament message (Mat. 28:19-22; Mark). The para-church emerges as a representation of being ministers in Christ demonstrating the diversity of Spirit-given gifts which enhances, even typifies the fundamental principle of edification of the body and service to the world.

Ministry of Evangelism through the Para-church

Most para-church associations concentrate principally on some form of evangelism or training for evangelism often with the incorporation of social services. These assembled bodies of believers, establish businesses, nonprofit corporations, private associations and volunteer societies to serve the cause of Christ. Christian para-church organizations include missions, youth associations, primary and secondary schools, colleges, universities; and counseling and social science associations. Christians innovatively construct what may be categorized by the para-church concept as a society for the promotion of Christianity, replete with seminaries, bookstores, television and radio stations, law firms; and health and human services groups. Scholarly exegesis and the significance of sound apologetics have encouraged para-church groups to develop schools of higher learning, supporting higher education for its Christian educators and leaders. This influence is seen as the universal Church heralds the good news through para-church groups to the available culture by various means affecting societal attitudes and "cultural forms such as legal codes, scientific treatise, social customs, educational systems, art and literary works."[17] Private schools have been established as a means of providing education that offers an alternative to secular schools. The developed curriculum is to inspire discipleship; and the advancement of the Gospel is its fundamental premise. Para-church groups, as independent agencies and Christ's ambassadors, form schools that strive in every aspect of its policies and practices to honor God using the Bible as the guide and rule for every area of philosophy and education. Consequentially, para-church organizations provide specific service and educational needs to local churches as seminars, conferences, published books, videos and computer technology made available through outsourcing to address underrepresented matters and to meet ministry goals. The message of the Gospel and its imperative to make disciples supports empowerment of the believer, aspiration for excellence in the dispersion of the gospel necessitating the edification and refinement of the people of God for ministry; and advances biblical support of cooperation between the church and the para-church.

INITIATED TO ADDRESS UN-CHURCHED COMMUNITIES

Aside from addressing the unmet or underrepresented issues of Christians, para-church organizations seek to expand the message of God to un-churched communities through declaration and service. According to the Barna Research group, un-churched is defined as an adult who has not attended a Christian church service within the past six months; excluding special services such as Easter, Christmas, weddings or funerals.[18] Barna reports that "one third of all adults remain un-churched as of 2005 and this number could reach nearly a million people annually."[19] Being un-churched does not insinuate non-Christian. More than three out of five un-churched adults consider themselves to be Christian and less than half claim they have made a personal commitment to Jesus Christ.[20] Being identified as un-churched constitutes not only church attendance but includes having limited or no personal relationship with God, experiencing no spiritual growth and unbelief. The para-church as an organized collaborative employs faith-guided, God-fearing individuals who engage in social welfare and evangelistic pursuits outside the walls of the local church particularly to the un-churched. These individuals or groups seek unity and cooperation within their ranks by advocating a shared spirituality that crosses denominational lines. They are often interdenominational entities, focusing on Christ, not on their separate church organizations with the capability of expanding God's message in unorthodox venues. With its broad categories of organizations such as: rescue missions, shelters to the transient, homeless, battered and abused; Christ-centered compassionate convalescent care and hospice care for the dying, organizations for feeding the hungry, discipling and psychosocial support, providing medical care and legal aid services for the indigent; and evangelism across the lifespan, the para-church is poised to carry out God's Great Commission meeting various human needs and directing people to Christ and His church; the biblical perspective supporting cooperation between the church and the para-church.

The capacity for person to person outreach for the local church has become limited due to migration of individuals, the development of wider geographical areas, cultural practices and philosophical differences. Therefore, the means to disseminate the gospel message has expanded through utilization of technology and mass media, often an innovation and resource of the para-church. According to the Barna Research Group, "more adults experience the Christian faith through Christian media such as radio, television, internet or books than attend Christian churches; and three-quarters of all churched adults supplement their church experience with exposure to media."[21] Para-church organizations emanated "in the form of interdenominational voluntary societies which are modifications of Christian orthodoxy and benevolent reform movements to attract un-churched and under-churched Americans."[22] In a society "draped in a dark time of spiritual chaos, where infidelity and indifference *or tolerance* threatens the very soul" of mankind, the para-church has developed and proliferated as a "solution to the dynamics of religious change" as a methodology to reach un-churched communities.[23] Its purpose is not to challenge the church but as directed by the message to the church and assigned by God, to be attentive to the un-churched.

The Para-church performs its Priestly ministry

The development of the para-church which is an enterprise of church members endeavoring in evangelistic pursuits, is predicated upon the biblical principle that every local church comprises a communal colony of believers who are a priesthood and directed to the service of restoring the Kingdom of God (I Tim. 4:1-5). The use of the term priest which was utilized to designate the special functional role depicted in the Old Testament appears as inconsistent to Christian leadership who argue against the autonomy of the para-church, though New Testament theology contends that every Christian is a priest and the human intermediary between God and man has been abolished in Jesus Christ, the eternal intercessor. Notably, the universal Church membership has been designated "a spiritual house, holy priesthood, to offer up spiritual sacrifices acceptable to God" (I Pet. 2:5; Rev. 1:6; 5:10; 20:6). Each individual believer, even the para-church, is admonished to self-sacrifice; and to be dedicated and prepared for God's service as a recognizable and attainable representation of worship (Rom. 12:1). The need to solve a problem, distribute information and offer creative methods to address societal needs is an expression of the role and the reason for the existence of para-church organizations. The Book of Jude affords support for the biblical perspective for cooperation between the church and the para-church; its attestation is that every believer must hold fast to the message of the Gospel and of necessity by the Spirit of the Gospel "snatch" the unbelieving and unrepentant soul from the eternal "fire." (Jude 23). It affirms that all believers are custodians of a common faith with divine appointment. Traditionally, a special class of individuals is expectantly responsible for the ministry of the local church and its surrounding community. The para-church erases the myth that a special class of individuals go into ministry. The Bible does not present a separate society of those who minister while others are expected to remain observers. There is no Scripture to enforce the notion that ministry is exclusive to professionals who have formal theological training or other distinctions.

The para-church providing service to the world is consignment to the biblical account of Jesus appointing and sending out His followers to "every town and place where He himself was going'" This is an acknowledgement that there were many outside of the faith to be reached, indicating an endeavor requiring much work and although many were being sent on this mission, still "the laborers were few" (Luke 10: 1-12). According to the Bible, every Christian is purposed for ministry. All disciples of

Christ are entrusted with stewardship of the souls of men (Luke 16:1-13). Consequently, the church functions to prepare the body of Christ for the task and responsibility of reaching the un-churched through service and evangelism. Saints engaged as the para-church, missionaries, volunteer charitable organizations or ministers of the gospel are instructed by the Word of God to form associations, friendships and develop relationships with the un-churched and introduce Christ. The church, guided by godly church leadership profits its ministry through the empowerment of its membership; the priesthood. The para-church exemplifies this membership meeting the physical needs of the poor, outcast and downtrodden and making practicalism in theology a priority (Rom. 15:27; James 2: 15-16).

Para-church Ministry enables the Church to be the Church

Societal transformation, with an increased capacity and desire for knowledge have produced new and innovative methods for delivering the fundamentals of the Christian faith. The effective ministry of the para-church enables the local church to be what God intends. The universal Church in contemporary society is becoming more acutely aware of the cultural realities of pluralism avowing normality with "its claims that the truths of the gospel be censured as imperialist and divisive as the expansion into modes of media such as radio, television, publishing and internet proliferates."[24] The influx of media exposure enables a greater reach for the dispersion of the gospel. The para-church flourishes predicated upon "competition from rivals *to Christianity* and intellectual convictions" which necessitates that the church determine alternative methodologies "and makes appropriate responses."[25] The local church has "the evangelical impulse to diligently seek to make the gospel accessible to strangers" and much like America in the late eighteenth century, "a religious free market exists.[26] Individuals can choose church or not; they can choose traditional religious beliefs or adopt one of the new religions being marketed. Churches compete with one another for members and those of more populist bent prosper."[27] Consequently the church must be mindful of its vulnerability and should not stop being the church to become "carried away by the error of unprincipled men; barely distinguishable from other goods and services providers, self-help groups and social organizations that make up the landscape of modern American life" (Gal. 6:1; II Pet. 3:17).[28] The para-church, the people of God, being empowered by the trainings of the church and assigned to be witnesses of Christ to the un-churched, has the capacity to engage various methodology to address societal discord and abate obscurity (Acts 1:8). The church of Christ has its mission to establish the Kingdom of God determined when "all reach unity in the faith" through the preparation and edification of the people of God as expressed in Scripture and is substantiation of the biblical perspective for cooperation between the church and the para-church (Eph. 5: 11-13).

Chapter Summary

Every believer is compelled to act according to the Spirit who works within "to will and to do according to God's purpose" (Phil. 2:14). Charles Spurgeon writes, "Jesus commands us to go into the entire world and preach the gospel to every creature; if we do what He commands us, the responsibility of the matter no longer rests with us." [29] This is affirmed in Mark 16:15 when Jesus responds affirmatively to His disciples regarding others outside of their ranks functioning in His name. Spurgeon contends that "a servant is not to justify his master's message, but to deliver it."[30] Every believer that is "called" and embraces the teachings of *the Word* is a disciple (John 6:65; 8:31). According to definition, a disciple is one who accepts and assists in disseminating the doctrines of another; a follower of a particular teacher or an adherent of certain principles which are maintained on the authority of the teacher. True discipleship is dependent upon the divine authority of Christ and not by human authority (John 8: 31; Mat. 15:19). Being fruitful workers, obedient and good stewards who acknowledge and accept the cost of discipleship is essential to being an effective disciple for the Lord (Mat. 7: 15-20, Mat. 25: 14-30; Luke 14: 25-35; John 15: 1-8). Jesus demonstrated during earthly interaction with His disciples that discipleship is an intensely personal experience of spiritual growth, character building and maturity in relationship with God. He requires that discipleship encompass an all importance in the life of believers, that spiritual maturity is developed prior to ministry and that the character expressed in the Word become the fruit of the individual's spirit prior to influence in the world. Every Christian has the awesome privilege and responsibility of expressing what it means to be in Christ, to walk in the Spirit and to live by faith, hence the insurgence of the para-church. The para-church has emerged as the evangelistic and discipleship portion of the church, organized independently, but not indiscriminately, as a recognizable group by their efforts to advance the Great Commission as Christ's disciples.

As identified in Scripture by the varied activities of the disciples such as Phillip, Paul, Peter, Ananias and other traveling ministers who functioned independent of a specified church, the para-church has existed in some form since the inception of Christianity (Acts 8: 26-35; 9:10, 33-39;10:17-23; 11: 19-24; III John). It is probable that the idiom or the prescribed use of the designation para-church referencing the people of God; the body of Christ and members of God's family is a misnomer. A legally accepted description alleges "the para-church is an independent and nonprofit organization that is religious, as evidenced by substantial religious qualities, and is not a church nor owned or operated by or solely affiliated with a local church."[31] The term is subtle and seditious, with its associative orientation as a supplementary ministry. The terminology is an assault on the doctrine of "one Lord, one faith, one body, one Spirit and one baptism" (Eph. 4:4-5). To state that the para-church exists to accomplish tasks the local church cannot, due to perceived or recognized deficiency; and is to work alongside or is subordinate to the church is a derogatory premise and an affront to the Word of God which supports cooperation and unity within the body of believers to function as ONE. Acknowledging that the Lord has assigned to each his task, the para-church as ambassadors in Christ evolved, *arguably*, as institutions to address underrepresented concerns and to address un-churched communities (I Cor. 3:5-9). Although they may, and indeed should work collaboratively with the local church, and according to the *Third Epistle of John*, receive its "hospitality," it may be required purposively or adventitiously, that the para-church remains self-governing (3-8).

This group of Christians emerged as disciples recognizing the necessity "to be defined by service and sacrifice" in Christ, for God's glory, rather than denomination or association.[32] According to Thomas Messner's article, "traditional religious organizations include churches and synagogues" and these organizations establish "secular, nonprofit activities and programs addressing spiritual and human services which they own, operate and make available to the public."[33] There is a concern that as "American religiosity becomes more pluralistic, more individualistic and more private; rather than occupying a central and influential place in people's lives, the local church is becoming increasingly marginalized."[34] As society experiences reallocation of priorities in its ethnic and cultural environment, the church should remain dominant in the lives of its membership; continuing to address "issues which are facts of everyday life for Christians," providing theological foundation, accountability and significance in God's plan of redemption for the world.[35] No one local church has the capability to assign all believers within the confines of their building; none have the means to meet all of the spiritual inspiration in the congregation or to address all of the necessities within the surrounding community. Scripture states that Jesus is the main foundation for the people of God and all are joined together in Him as His body, "created in Christ Jesus for good works, which God prepared beforehand that we should walk in them" (John 15:5; Eph. 2:10; 4:5-6). Is Christ divided? The para-church comprises disciples of Christ performing priestly ministry according to the Word of God. Its conception is an attempt to respond to people as instructed by Jesus: meeting people within their own environment, seeing people as they are without partiality or judgment and addressing their needs affording further support for cooperation between the church and the para-church.

CHAPTER 4

THE CONTROVERSY: LOCAL CHURCH PERSPECTIVE ON THE PARA CHURCH

The Church is a living organism produced to receive its commands from its Originator. It is an organism with a purpose and as an organism the Church has transcendent and dynamic qualities. These qualities are often observed as the church advances to accomplish its preordained mission as a "called and separated assembly of born-again Christians" who are God's tools "to call out of the many nations, a people for His name" (Acts 15:14).[1] "The church is the context, the environment, in which Christian growth is nurtured through worship, fellowship, teaching, witness and service."[2] Significantly, it is to be "the grace and humility of Christ;" the model of selfless ministry in the body (Phil. 2: 1-13).[3] The New Testament apostolic church primarily focused its missions on "how they should relate to the societies and cultures in which they were individually located rather than how to address foreign societies and cultures," [4] To disseminate the Gospel there were members of this early church who were missionary-minded proclaiming Jesus and His teachings throughout the various geographical regions. Textual analysis infers that following the acceptance of Christianity by Constantinople and the Roman Empire, the church redirected its focus of mission activity exclusively toward "alien societies and cultures and ceased to be concerned with relations between the church and its home environment."[5]

Worldwide missions developed as an endeavor to make disciples of nations that existed outside of the normal outreach responsibilities of the local church. A mission defined is a ministry commissioned by a religious organization to propagate its faith or carry out humanitarian work. Para-church missions comprised ministries involving a social, economical and spiritual service inclusive of the local community or culture.[6] The para-church, as a mission, creates tension for the local church due to anonymity and autonomy. The most significant controversial paradigm that infuses differences between the local church and the para-church is whether both agree that each comprise membership as the body of Christ. For the local church spiritual and logical deductions from Scriptural passages command discipleship under its authority and propel the feasibility for antagonism against the existence of para-church organizations. Interpretation of the various biblical epistles to the churches consigns the offices of pastor, teacher and evangelist solely to the local church and is distinguished as a system of government expressly for the local church without regard for the universality and dynamic qualities of the Church proposed in Scripture. This hierarchical perspective causes further discord as church leadership dissuades the evangelistic and disciple-making pursuits of its congregation and the para-church. In spite of this adversity the para-church who are believers and each individually members of the organism called Church, pursues God's mandate to "go, make disciples and train in spiritual truths" (Mat. 28: 19; Mark 16: 15; Luke 24:47-48).

A long history of intense conflict based on personal beliefs and religious ideologies has been demonstrated in literature. The perspective of the local church on the para-church is exemplified as a paradoxical relationship or the absence of relationship between them and presents many difficulties in the analysis of the controversy. This illumines the antagonistic perspective of the local church which bespeaks a theological and institutional divide and elicits disagreements over doctrines that obscure the biblical principle of unity in the body of Christ. "Far from being a peripheral, optional doctrine and relationship, the reality of the church and the obligation of Christians to be part of it are essential New Testament teaching."[7] The local church is where the believer goes for fellowship, to hear about Jesus, learn of God, to worship the Father, and commune with Him. Every believer constitutes the body of Christ, the Church. According to Mikolaski, "while the apostles were regarded as the pillars of every church, other ministries and offices developed through the extension and universalizing of the gospel."[8] The assignment given by God to members of each church makes it a distinctive community distinguished as multiple composites with one mission.

THEOLOGICAL DIVIDE

The controversy between the church and the para-church is predicated upon a theological divide. To ascertain the doctrinal perspective fueling this controversy at issue is the theological divide relative to the role and responsibility of the local church pertaining to its relationship to believers and nonbelievers. The ancient history of Judaism managed to ignore or avoid unbelievers as an anomaly. The perception was that unbelieving Gentiles were idolaters and the rationale was that idolatry was akin to uncleanness, which according to Jewish law required avoidance. Their belief was to expect that God would resolve the unbeliever's situation therefore, the religious community's focus was on the elect, establishing the identified distinction between Israel and the Gentiles. Christianity embodies a relationship of identity between itself and Judaism. "The salvation effected in Christ is uniquely comprehended by means of Scripture, where Scripture refers to the canon of Israel."[9] "The early Christian Church which was Jewish, conservative, legalistic and conscious of its own authority" worshipped in temples and synagogues, fulfilled the Law of Moses, shared goods within its community and celebrated the Eucharist.[10] The New Testament demonstrates the Great Commission as its evangelical influence and the rationale for presenting the gospel of salvation to all mankind. This means that unlike the Judaism concept of avoidance and separation from nonbelievers God ordained disciples to establish a communal colony (the church) of His chosen children. Theologically, each local church identifies itself as the direct means of evangelism to believers and nonbelievers. This fuels the adversarial response toward the para-church. Proponents of this concept assert that the role and responsibility of the church is to delegate messengers, prophets, leaders, ministers, evangelists and missionaries into the world. The philosophy behind this point of view is that the maintenance of correct theology and effectiveness in evangelism requires direct appeal for repentance and conversion from appointed ministers of the gospel who are specifically aligned with and representative of a particular church. The contention is the Bible imparts that specified individuals from the local community who were apostles preached the gospel, admonished repentance for the conversion of Jews and Gentiles, established the local church and directed its membership. According to this perspective, there is no basis for an enterprise which is autonomous with the capacity to function independent of the church. Consequently, the church views the para-church as deliberately defiant, apostate and an assault on Christianity.

The Para-church is Unbiblical

The Word of God through the Spirit of God is designed to convert the hearer, which is in opposition to traditional Jewish philosophy. The Jewish law is generally interpreted as opposed to proselytizing and religious conversion of nonbelievers is discouraged. In the New Testament, Paul's epistles represent an attempt to accomplish a coherent vision for Jews and Gentiles. He argued that "salvation is offered and granted to both Jews and Gentiles as children of promise, severing the gospel from its Judaic roots" of separation and avoidance.[11] Each local church is presented in the Scriptures as individual communities having the same purpose and each is observed as being formulated by the same Truth. The church as a universal body is concerned with the restoration of men and women to God. For the believer, the church is more than an institution. It is a complex, powerful unifying body "committed to the gospel, the lordship of Jesus Christ and the fellowship of the saints locally."[12] "It is entrusted with the word of Christ's gospel generating a new people to go out into the world with a new outlook on life while having in view His return and His Kingdom" inferring that the biblical perspective supports cooperation between the church and the para-church (Luke 24:44-48; Rom. 5:1-5;8:23-26; I Thess. 4:16-18; 5:23; Heb, 12:1-2; 13:20-21;James 5:7-8; I Pet. 4:17-19).[13]

The local church has the uniqueness of being an assembly where believers receive the zeal to communicate the gospel with unbelievers; and governed by THE Divine Authority, the church is to demonstrate impartiality in its efforts to empower the saints for service. Although comprised of believers, the para-church, presents as perilous to the church provoking animosity. Based on the doctrinal perspective of some church leaders the para-church is determined to be unbiblical due to its self-governance and therefore, separated from the authority of the church. Church leaders have asserted that there is no theological foundation for any organizational structure besides the church and that the para-church is unbiblical on the basis that it lacks accountability to the church. Church leaders with the perspective of the local church having an authoritative stance, view the para-church as disobedient to the Word of God alleging the local church has the God ordained authority over all Christian activities. One prevailing argument for this assertion is that the apostles who were with Christ founded churches, formed local assemblies of the converted; and assigned qualified men to guide, rule and shepherd the community of believers and the contention is that no other organization appears in the New Testament. Therefore, the para-church is distinguished as "undermining the corporate power and authority of the church" and its effectiveness.[14] The viewpoint that para-church organizations established by biblical principles under God's authority are unbiblical is an audacious perspective considering the content of the New Testament recognizing all believers as separately answerable to God in Christ and its explication of Christ as the single authority of the church.

The Para-church Compromises the Gospel

A local church perspective on the para-church which promotes controversy is its concept that while endeavoring to engage constituents and clients the para-church compromises the Gospel. According to opponents of the para-church, the problem is not simply ecclesiological but ecclesial. To the local church it is more than a matter of church constitution, it is a matter regarding the doctrine of Christianity; the very essence of the church. This perspective presupposes that the para-church is tantamount to heresy. Heresy implies distinction between the foundational Christian beliefs of the church and the para-church. Literature suggests that as the Christian church has become more organized, recognized and accepted, those who fail to uphold the orthodoxy is theorized to compromise its message, are considered heretics and enemies of the accepted order. The implication is that to the church the para-church appears to lack conformity to the approved form of Christian doctrine, philosophy and ideology. Its modes of conduct are considered uncharacteristic of the acceptable behaviors, attitudes or beliefs of the conventional local church. Subsequently, the nontraditional methodologies and unorthodox perspectives of the para-church demonstrates blatant refusal to adhere to acceptable, traditional and established religious customs. Therefore, it is decidedly reviled and characterized as antagonistic to the faith, as accommodating to a secular worldview, an endangerment to the reputation of the church and the integrity of the Gospel.

As the para-church endeavors to disseminate the message of Christ it seeks to permeate a society of multiple cultural and religious perspectives, with less constraint than the local church, it encounters many opportunities to penetrate this world relying on biblical truths. Armed with the knowledge that in Christ there is liberty, these disciples, in effect "become a slave," as stated by the apostle Paul; in the Great Commission of Christ (I Cor. 9:19-23). The para-church as an assembled community of God's people often of diverse backgrounds, in its efforts to engage society *having the mind of Christ* and awareness of interaction with human culture, ideology, social and political systems are touted by the local church as heretics who compromise the gospel. The social aspects which are a component of para-church evangelistic ministry such as providing for the poor, widowed and oppressed are considered by the church as propaganda for self-serving purposes regardless of the outcry of divine intent, theological basis and biblical content. Scripture affirms that each member of the body of Christ have at their disposal the incentive of the Holy Spirit for evangelism and discipleship without compromise. However, resultant projects being administered without "deliberation and the consent of the established church authorities" causes dissension as being irrespective of established orthodoxy.[15]

The Para-church is Commercialism

The theological divide comprises ethical perspectives inclusive of commercialism and competition. Commercialism is defined as practices, methods, or purposes that involve the exchange of goods and services or the exploitation of intangibles for private gain. It appears to the local church that the para-church has a private agenda or spirit not in harmony with the mission of the church and therefore, is a liability instead of a supportive asset. The assertion is compounded with newly created innovative organizations and practices emphasizing "human instrumentality" which without censor by the church elicits encroachment and a violation of the "expressed dictates of Scripture."[16] The para-church is viewed by the church as secularized business ventures disguised as associations and volunteer societies. Although the predominance of commercialism in the body of Christ may be observed as the local church succumbs to the rigors of the contemporary marketplace demonstrative of rival companies rather than public utilities. The church perspective is that the para-church as an autonomous enterprise creates marginalization of religion and increasingly causes disconnect through dissimilar intentions distinguished from religious norms which detract quality, value and reputation from the church. The perception is that the promotion of para-church organizations is evidence of a decline in religious beliefs and practices. There is consensus that the task for the church includes engagement with the world for evangelism but the methodologies are not often distinct or resources available. Evangelistic activity is commonplace in the church as the presentation of the gospel through invitation to conversion, followed by initiation into the family of God. "The aim of the local church is to introduce persons into the life and mission of its Christian community and to assist them to become responsible participants" in the building of God's Kingdom.[17]

Evangelism is an integral part of the requisite participatory task of the entire body of Christ. It may be "defined as member recruitment" or message marketing and has been mandated for all disciples.[18] The para-church is recognized by some church leaders as a representative group of Christ's disciples functioning according to the commission of God, but for financial gain. It is a reality that the para-church, much like the church, has to concentrate on the expense of maintaining the organization which may divert attention from the primary purpose for which it was instituted. Therefore, the para-church must exercise caution for fear of alienating the constituency to whom they look for financial support. Strategies developed and implemented by para church groups for evangelism requires imaginative tactics and pioneering not endorsed by the church enabling the para-church to initiate relationships which foster the presentation of the gospel (I Cor. 9:19-23; Phil. 2:5-7). An argument of church leaders is that in its delivery of innovative evangelistic projects, the para-church must be subordinate to societal restrictions and laws much like commercial enterprise, rather than the Scriptures. The para-church, much like any Christian institution, group or individual, must evaluate every affiliation through a biblical lens and uphold its criteria of morality as chosen ambassadors entrusted with the power of God (II Cor. 4:7). The para-church furnishes opportunity for an initial substantive interaction and relationship through diverse modalities. This notion of evangelism perpetuates the idea of commercialism because the local church purports that evangelism is being utilized as an aspect of marketing secularism or politicizing Christ. This implies an ideology of materialism, individual interest and personal ownership conceptualized as services for acquisition rather than spiritual investiture. Through the lens of the church the para-church "is seen as an initiative manifesting the entrepreneurial nature" and following the edict of society.[19]

The Para-church is Competition

The para-church is vehemently opposed by the church as an attempt to establish new religious institutions and methods for what has been deemed the function of the local church. Church leadership who oppose the para-church protests ecumenism, view Christians without authorization meeting in non-church settings as abandonment of tradition and threatening to the centrality and existence of the local church. Controversy between the church and the para-church is regarded as competition which may be identified as concerns that para-church organizations interfere with church ministry, induce people to waiver in their commitment and potential leadership is redirected from local churches. Historically, laity compelled to minister has found recourse outside of the local church. The Scriptures provide insights into God's sovereignty and explicates that God chooses His people from among Jews and Gentiles eliciting an appreciation for the argument that God's plan may be offensive to those who imagine they are in an unquestioned position of authority when in fact they are required to co-exist with the unsuspected (Rom. 9; Mat.19:30; Mark 10:42-45). The relationship between the church and the para-church is highly complex in view of the fact that their foundational differences rests on the components of varying perspectives derived from biblical faith, theological primacy and sociological contextualization. It has been alleged that the controversy is affirmed as an "environmental catastrophe" within the community of believers "attributable to an exaggeration of human authority and control coupled with rejection and accountability to God."[20] Christian churches are divided into thousands of competing and sometimes antagonistic camps and these "have to compete with followers of other non-Christian groups."[21] Although autonomous, anomalous and purposeful the para-church though distinct from the church and perceived as competition is often affiliated with the church through its membership. The Bible supports cooperation between the church and the para-church in its pronouncement that the oversight of legitimate activities pertaining to its constituency is the responsibility of the church under the supervision of its elders as God's stewards (Acts 20:28). Consequentially, competition produces pathological relations due to "alienation from the Source of the true being and reality" from which the para-church derives its existence (Acts 20:28; Titus 1:7; I Pet. 5:1-3).[22] "Is Christ divided" (I Cor. 1:13)? The church proclaims that the para- church, by its existence and practice is threatening. Every believer is a part of the body of Christ. Variance of location, practice, organizational structure and position should not override the unity of the body of Christ espoused in biblical doctrine. It is perilous when structure, position, title and presumed authority elicit more loyalty than God (Mat. 23:8-10). The church and the para-church must of necessity find balance between wisdom and vulnerability to accomplish God's work (Mat. 10:16). Competition in the body of Christ at any level indicates "lost sight of being for Jesus."[23]

INSTITUTIONAL DIVIDE

An institutional divide between the church and the para-church emphasizes structural perspectives as an organization. Church leadership argues that by its nature the para-church is apostate being ecumenical, having a more social context and lacking jurisdiction by the local church. Evangelism and social concerns are sometimes seen as mutually exclusive which reinforces the assertion of the local church that the para-church compromises the gospel. The term apostasy means revolt, indicating that the members of the body of Christ associated with the para-church are defectors; abandoning tradition and hierarchical lines of authority. A few of the identified issues surround arguments such as: the para-church is not affiliated with a particular denomination, being ecumenical para-church organizations do not involve the kind of people with whom the local church is accustomed to associating; the para-church doesn't do things the way the church is accustomed to doing them or the church, denomination or association won't get the recognition. Brackney has defined the local church as "a social institution, hierarchically organized, autonomous and served by a professional priesthood."[24] Also defined as an edifice, it is the place for learning, acceptance, development, growth, maturity and disciple-making. Within this edifice the local church community immerse themselves in the brotherhood of the saints as they worship, pray and expand their capacities to fulfill the purposes of God. Considered apostate by the church, the para-church is viewed by church leadership as an aversion and challenges its existence. Predicated upon Scripture, these challenges include denial of the truth, betrayal of Christian faith, false teachers, dubious motives and rivalry (II Cor. 11:3; II Pet. 2:1-3).[25] The para-church charges that the Word of God exhorts every believer to be guided by the Holy Spirit in decision making having the willingness to listen, discern truths and obey God's Word (Prov. 3:5-6; Gal. 5:14-18). God's Word establishes that: the body of Christ must *be fruitful and multiply* and test the spirits recalling Jesus' declaration that "he who is not against us is for us" and no one comes into the family of God but by His grace (Mark 9:40; John 14:6; Rom.10:11-13; 15:1-7; I Cor. 12:4-6; Eph 4:1-3; I John 4:1). Is Christ divided? In Christ there is no subordinate, but there is legitimacy in Him; to combat disorder, disunity and dissension.

The Para-church is Insubordinate

The parable of the tenants in Matthew 21 provides support for the biblical perspective of cooperation between the church and the para-church in its depiction of one servant community. The primary subject of this parable is to the address the Jewish community's persecution and refusal to accept Jesus as the Son of God and the anticipated Messiah. Jesus furnishes a unique look at the structural perspective of the church and the para-church demonstrated as servants of the same Master and in existence for His purpose. Tenants were entrusted by the landowner with the management of his vineyard to produce fruit for his benefit. The tenants concurred with the Landlord in the beginning; agreeing to the relationship. When the time for harvesting came, the Landowner sent His servants to get His fruit. These servants belonged to the landowner, but were not necessarily of this particular vineyard. This is analogous to the para-church who are members of the body of Christ, servants of the Master to assist in His ministry heralding from different churches. In this parable, the landlord's servants served to remind the tenants of their role and responsibilities, to acknowledge the day of recompense and to assist with the ingathering. The tenants who managed the vineyard designed to preserve all of the wealth and grandeur for themselves. Although the servants came as representatives of the Master and spoke in His name, they were not received by the tenants. They were persecuted, treated cruelly, sorely despised, reproached, exiled and punished unto death. The Master offered many opportunities for repentance and restoration of the previous relationship sending multiple messages, even his son. The tenants determined that the Master's son was a hindrance to their personal goals disposed of him. The tenants became the enemy of the servants, the Son and the Master.

This is the message of the cross and a blueprint which necessitates interrelationship of the Lord's people. Notwithstanding any demographic, in this case status, all were assigned a task by the Master; each obliged to be accepted, allowed to function within their particular task and demonstrate love for one another. The message of the cross is that in the final hour, God, the Master, sent forth His Son to sacrifice His life and correct the wrong as a demonstration of the love of God. Disobedience to the Christian doctrine of love one to another is akin to rejecting the chief cornerstone.

Referencing the church-para-church controversy, it is a reminder that God is Lord of the church, all of the resources are His and this parable illustrates that those entrusted with His church have no claim on God's heritage. Individuals in authority of the church are not to lord over those with ostensibly less authority (I Pet. 5:1-3). The concept of subordination is problematic since it so often elicits sovereignty. This parable reiterates the necessity for mutuality and cooperation between all believers in God's plan of kingdom building.

"That which makes the para-church such a lightening rod of controversy is that its subordinate role is often questionable."[26] The local church perspective on the para-church which promotes controversy entails the hierarchical concept that each local church is the sole *gateway* to the kingdom of God and leadership of the church are the *gatekeepers* with the sole responsibility for the activities of the body of Christ. The gatekeepers' responsibility includes proclamation of the gospel of Christ, exhortation of personal conversion and growth within the church community. The discord evident in the body of Christ establishes that a human perspective instead of a biblical perspective on authority and the responsibility of every believer divulges a problematic construct "as one of the authorities insists that their authority has preeminence."[27] The local church is not recognized by the para-church as the absolute authority. Therefore, the para-church is distinguished as "undermining the corporate power and authority of the church and exemplified as insubordinate."[28] Para-church leadership acknowledges its capacity as afforded by the consummate authority of God expounded in Scripture. The controversy in some Christian communities surrounding the autonomy of the para-church is accounted as appropriating the authority of the church which often advocates division, differentiation and delineation. The institutional contention is that "the sole source for the propagation of the gospel is the church established by Christ as governed according to Scripture; not para-church societies established by men."[29] As a result of consigned incongruity the indication is that the para-church does not merit recognition as an affiliate of the church. This incites confusion in the body of Christ as its legitimacy; efforts to assuage human suffering and proliferation of the gospel message are questioned. There is a lack of support from local church leadership regarding the para-church that consequently causes an immense degree of caution in church membership who are censored or discern the questionable church-para-church relationship. As the para-church pursues "ministry beyond the walls of the traditional church, many are cautiously accepted by some

Christians, but with unvoiced guilt."[30] The local church-para-church controversy raises contention on what constitutes the biblical expression of the New Testament Church when the rationale for the disunity between them represents that the local church references itself as a requisite to relationship with the Lord.

The Para-church is Illegitimate

The church does not recognize the legitimacy of the para-church. Each aggregate staunchly maintains its sodality as a denomination, association or assembly. Each credit the Scriptures for their authoritarianism; giving attention to written cannons and codes of conduct which expressly disallow participation with others outside of a particular religious establishment even while both profess faith in Christ. Each avows all religious opinions which deny a doctrine different than their own as heresy. "Each congregation is focused on its own membership, not as a community of disciples making disciples but as a collection of individuals whose concern is largely their own group."[31] This in effect is troublesome for the para-church who are often individuals within these congregations aspiring to answer the call of God in their lives, inhibited by church leadership, caught in the confusion, isolationism and separation of the body of Christ. Consenting to the authority of church leaders often requires unqualified submission of the para-church without individual freedom of thought or action. Disagreements over doctrines of law and grace obscure the biblical principle of unity in the body of Christ, who are individually and collectively children of God.

Labeling the para-church as apostate is a parody. The biblical accounts of apostasy are demonstrations of turning away from original faith and beliefs toward another which is not occurring with the para-church (Gal 4:8-10; I Tim 4:1-32; Heb. 6:4-6; II Pet 2:20-21). The notion of defection incites severe opposition and criticism from the church. However, societal outreach is mitigated due to schisms and disassociations between churches, denominations, associations and para-church groups. The para-church is eminently ecumenical, not apostate; the local church is conspicuously denominational, even when labeled nondenominational. Ecumenicalism, under the auspices of Christianity is the engagement of individuals in varied collaborations, although separate according to religious history, doctrine and practice. Ecumenicalism is categorized with apostasy by the local church, accompanied by disdain and efforts which promote it are frequently undermined by religious tradition and laws that preference estrangement over the communion of believers espoused in Scripture (John17: 20-26; Phil. 2:1-4). Ecumenicalism is dismissed as illegitimacy. There is a belief that ecumenicalism has a causal effect within the para-church. Local church perspective is the para-church loosely regards the essential doctrinal foundation of Christianity creating a causal effect to further aggravate relations within the body of Christ which manifests as a culture of isolationism, secularism and plurality inducing an increasingly combative ecclesiastical community. The church invalidates the para-church based on contextual traditions, prejudices and possible misunderstandings, promoting criticality and discord. The Bible commands love for each other as disciples of Christ (John 13:34-35). Criticality and discord is not motivated by love. It indicates that instead of the church seeing through the eyes of grace, it is seeing through the lens of law.

The Para-church is Consumerism

The emergence of the para-church is theorized to have proliferated based on the dictates of population, community and society with the ensuing combination of opportunities and individuals guided by the Spirit. The church deems that the para-church has material acquisition as its focus and contends that preoccupation with consumerism engenders an institutional divide. Church leaders contend that the para-church demonstrates acquisitiveness and obsession with money, acquiescing to various schemes that are a violation to the sanctity of Christianity such as: "breaking commands by Christ not to be concerned with worldly pursuits and attainments, merchandising the gospel and reducing the gospel to a commodity to be traded"[32] The presumption is para-church organizations employ policies which allow all paying individuals membership regardless of religious commitment. Based upon the perspective regarding the illegitimacy of the para-church the church admonishes its members to view the para-church from a consumerist orientation. The result is the church-para-church controversy. Given the hierarchical arrangement of the church individuals with authority assume the right to issue commands subordinates perceive as obligations to obey. The economic agenda of this era has an incapacitating effect on the local church; and the para-church's need of resources from local church membership causes further or continued division. Church leaders determine that the para-church usurps authority, human and financial resources from the church. Economic constraints may be partially due to the divided mindset of the church. In recent history, the appeal of nonreligious, charitable, social institutions has been answered through contributions by church members. Currently congregants contributing resource support to agencies accomplishing specialized missions on behalf of the universal Church of Christ is "off-putting" to local church leadership and is seen as "undermining denominational and theological heritages."[33] As contemporary society promotes individual prosperity and the church observes increased competition for funds, church leadership becomes less mission-minded urging the assembled body of Christ to reduce or eliminate endorsements and contributions.[34] Even examining contributions afforded the church, individual and corporate financial "behaviors are closely tied to a worldly economic structure."[35] The church functions within, what is referred to by Weber as the spirit of capitalism demonstrating preoccupation with self; and the acquisition and accumulation of wealth is in stark contrast to biblical accounts which "characterize the striving for profit as moral turpitude."[36] In this predominantly sectarian climate both the church and the para-church must take care not to manipulate individuals through pressure techniques or become unduly preoccupied with statistics, finances and competition.

The para-church is poised to address secularism, individualism and pragmatism in preparation for the church and the Kingdom of God analogous to John the Baptist who addressed impropriety and fostering relationship with God as he prepared the way for Jesus. The church asserts that the para-church having a penchant for consumerism institutes "new linguistic orthodoxies in the name of pluralism, inclusivity" and the pressures of society.[37] Many para- church organizations are limited, shackled and sometimes doomed to failure encumbered by lack of financial support from the local church. The para-church seeks remedy for insubstantial resources from various institutions, foundations and individuals. This is construed by the church as a violation of the institution of Christianity since para-church organizations function within parameters established by the various contributors often based on specific program guidelines not the foundational messages of the Bible. The argument of church leaders is that the para-church as consumerists must be subordinate to secular propositions. The church contends that with its consumerist orientation and conciliatory behaviors the para-church readily relinquishes its doctrinal and organizational authority. They assert that this perspective influences the organization's goals, strategies and affiliations toward lucrative partners; sacrificing the gospel and forbidding any societal usefulness to promote the glory of God. Opponents of the para-church reference the Second

Letter of Peter as a basis for their opposition claiming that the para-church is illegitimate because the church has been given everything needed to function as the glorious body of Christ and does not need *outside* help. This proposition truly has a self-centered connotation. Peter's second letter to the churches endorses the biblical perspective of cooperation between the church and the para-church with its "Christ-centered thinking directed toward God-centered living emphasizing the need of every believer to be zealous for God's purposes." [38]

Chapter Summary

The Christian style of life is to be expressed as service in pursuit of mercy, justice and peace with the goal to thrive in anticipation of a promised future Kingdom. The Bible provides principles that are to be evident by Church membership in the world and within the local church community. The church functions within a designed, determined and tried set of rules, traditions, procedures and expectations. Its organizational structure is intended for ministering and mentoring the saints of God. This is where the Word of God is preached, the sacraments are offered and congregations of believers are disciplined. On the other hand, the para-church is structured through faith, innovation and idealism. The notion is to be the biblical standard in an unbelieving world and engage others exemplified through various efforts of mission. Although the literal word para-church is not written in the Bible, the para-church attempts to be recognized as the biblically distinguished universal Church engaging in evangelism and discipleship. Its existence and authoritative disconnect causes controversy for the local church. "The para-church is considered by church leadership to be guided by an independent spirit of narcissism or humanism; the desire for self-direction without accountability." [39] The church, as the body of Christian believers, has determined that the para-church is heresy, illegitimate and apostasy. It is deemed unbiblical, due to lack of conformity to the approved Christian doctrine, philosophy, hierarchy and ideology. Their modes of conduct are considered uncharacteristic of the acceptable behaviors, beliefs or attitudes of the conventional local church. Church leadership attests that the para-church is governed by finance and this necessitates compromise of biblical principles and the gospel message.

The question of legitimacy and competitive perspectives causes church leadership to renounce any support by its membership. The constituents of the para-church, being Spirit-guided members of the body of Christ are constrained to facilitate their assigned task. The parable of the talents illustrates the necessity of industriousness and the legitimacy of practices involving commerce to advantage Kingdom building superseding personal gain (Mat. 25:14-30). The multiplicity of local churches and denominations absorb human and financial resources that could be shared for effective service and evangelism. The reality is that apart from God establishing believers the church and the para-church would cease to exist.

Scripture is inspired by God as a pattern for believers in all churches; all have been purchased with the blood of the lamb (Acts 20:28). The local assembly of believers has the governance of overseers who are to "shepherd the flock, not as lords over God's heritage, but being examples to them" (I Pet. 5:1-4; Mat.21:33-45).[40] The overseer is not the owner of the flock but is compensated, having assigned authority to be responsible to guide, guard and nourish the flock on behalf of another; necessitating humility in execution. Ultimately it is God who validates functions performed, recognized roles and delegated assignments for His purpose. Jerry White states that "in the New Testament the main application of authority is in the area of personal life and discipline, not ministry."[41] The Scriptures inform us that Jesus, though God Himself, did not exalt Himself as God, but humbled Himself even unto the stature and status of humanity (Phil. 2: 6-8). Jesus is presented as the authority; having authority over life and death, authority as the Son of God who always has the Father's ear and does the Father's bidding (John 11:42). His mission was fulfillment of the law to which mankind is unable to fully adhere; and having been "given all authority" from the Father, to restore humanity to its initial relationship with Him (John 11; Mat. 28:19). Jesus as head of the church and the example to mankind as the greatest authority demonstrated that every action which He performed was instigated by an underlying motivation to serve God and humanity. His actions present a more balanced perspective on the subject of authority. As we ponder the evidence in the New Testament establishing the church and its depiction of Jesus as the only authority, we ascertain that authority affords the ideological perception of a function being performed or a recognized role of responsibility rather than an office or position. Other than Christ, Scripture does not engender or falsely ennoble any particular individual or entity, for Scripture purports that every believer is a bondservant for the Lord and "should not think of themselves highly" (Col. 1:16-18). To affirm the need for cooperation between the church and the para-church the New Testament teaches that all members are important, are expected to serve and should be honored as they do so. Various gifts and roles are to "edify the body, to extend Christ's mission of service to the world, and bring honor to God" in the world.[42] The Bible contends that Christ is the incontrovertible authority of the church. He is the disciple of disciples yet He made authority of no consequence; only God's will. All Christian churches are local assemblies of believers and therefore components, individually and collectively, of the One body which is under Christ's authority. Every believer shall be required to give an individual account to Christ. This eradicates the concept of an unquestionable chain of command although the relational bond of the communal colony affirms the necessity of willing submission and respect of the conscience of one another (Rom. 14:21-23; Heb. 12:17). Israel Selvanayagam offers insight on this and the biblical support for cooperation between the church and the para-church:

There are things hidden and they belong to the Lord our God, but what is revealed belongs to us and our children forever; it is for us to observe all that is prescribed in the law (Deut. 29:29). One can add more dimensions of this law, the scope of which has never been restricted. We have more than sufficient inspiration and guidance to adore God in freedom and love and to work vigorously for a better society with justice, peace and integrity of creation. The death and resurrection of Jesus is a historical attestation of the struggle for life and promise of a hopeful future. We don't claim that we know everything. At present we see only puzzling reflections in a mirror, but one day we shall see face to face (I Cor. 13:12). We still need to attain to the unity inherent in our faith and in our knowledge of the Son of God—to mature manhood, measured by nothing less than the full stature of Christ (Eph. 4:13).[43]

The multiplicity of highly organized denominations, doctrinal controversies, church-affiliated for-profit agencies and nonprofit missions present a dynamic movement within the church, proliferating disunity and frustration in the body of believers which goes unnoticed; while the stream of controversy surrounding the institution of para-church organizations is exacerbated. Much like other human traditions enmeshed in dissonance and battle, if it persists, strife among the brethren will likely lead to ruin. Is Christ divided? The embittered assertions of the church toward the para-church are threatening to the body of Christ as believers become enslaved by *spiritual warfare* and nonbelievers are consoled by their animosity.

CHAPTER 5

THE INTEGRAL RELATIONSHIP BETWEEN THE CHURCH AND THE PARA CHURCH

The language of the New Testament purposed the church as an assembly or citizens called to assemble. It is also translated as congregation and has incurred an additional meaning as a community with shared beliefs. The Greek word ekklesia has the direct denotation of *call out* or summon. As members of this community of the summoned, the para-church has a conferred covenantal relationship in Christ with the church through the Holy Spirit. Rational inquiry regarding the authority of Scriptures relative to the local church entails a historical and theological anomaly: is the Holy Bible the written component of a synoptic revelation entrusted to the church and therefore to be interpreted within the context of the local church perspective or is the Holy Bible the revealed Word of God; and the church is to be defined as a collective who claim adherence to this revelation? According to Scripture, every believer has the manifestation of the Spirit accompanied by gifting and these gifts are at the discretion of the Father (I Cor. 12:7). Scripture states that "there is only one God, one baptism and one Spirit which is in all; and a house divided cannot stand" (Luke 11:17; Eph. 4. 4-5). Is Christ divided? Paul cautions every believer "that there may be no divisions among you and that you may be perfectly united in mind and thought" (I Cor. 1:10). There is never reference to the individual performing the baptism, the geographical location or the church to which the person joins; every believer's union is in Christ alone.

The unification of the church and the para-church as one body in God's purpose is expounded by a biblically sanctioned servant relationship in Christ. This servant relationship, due to its corresponding reciprocity, implies that a higher cost of self-denial is required to inhibit church comprehension that theologically it has priority and dominancy. Christ demonstrates leadership of His church by "becoming the servant of all; power is discovered in submission and the foremost symbol of this radical servanthood is the cross."[1] There is an attempt by para-church organizations to avoid encroaching on the traditional roles and hierarchical arrangements of the church. The deliberate act of omission by the church often causes para-church leadership "to be defensive and to explain why they chose to minister independently of the traditional church."[2] However, as Wilmer asserts, Christians make the mistake of limiting God when it is assumed that God only performs His work through the traditional church, a specific denomination or judicatory.[3] The term para-church has been adopted to mean any spiritual-based ministry whose organization is not under the control or authority of a local congregation, denomination or association. The biblical perspective which supports cooperation between the local church and the para-church alleges that every child of God are in a relationship of service to God and each other through Jesus Christ.

According to the Scriptures the church has a unique characteristic. It is a complex organism or system having properties and functions determined not only by its parts and the relations of its individual parts, but by the character of the whole that they compose and by the relations of the parts to the whole (I Cor.12). The distinctive qualities of the parts in reference to the whole enable the efforts of both to be effective. Rick Warren states that "the greatest need" in Christian churches "is the release of members for service.[4] Each member is interrelated as children of God. Constituents of para-church organizations are representatives of a local church regardless of expedition. This is depicted in Scripture by the missionary journeys of Paul and by Phoebe who traveled from Greece to Rome in service for the Lord (Rom.16:1-2). The interconnectedness of the individual to the church warrants "an intentional, well-planned system for uncovering, mobilizing and supporting the giftedness of its members."[5] According to Scripture, each member is "God's workmanship, created in Christ Jesus to do good works, which God prepared in advance to" be performed (Eph. 2: 10). This indicates that God has a design for every believer and every believer, born of the Spirit, has a responsibility to be directed by His will and unified in Christ. There are no insignificant ministries imposed by the Holy Spirit.

This principle presents a biblical basis which supports cooperation between the church and the para-church. It is imperative that both entities recognize the role each orchestrates as the body of Christ (I Cor. 12: 18-22).

COVENANTAL RELATIONSHIP

The integral relationship between the church and the para-church is established by God as a covenantal relationship. This covenantal relationship which revealed the chosen people of God was announced in the Old Testament through the circumcision. Scripture emphasizes in the New Testament that an internal circumcision must occur in the heart of the elect and is demonstrated as unity, love and respect (Rom. 2:28-29). Enmity within the body of Christ is to be abolished by the blood of Jesus "for He Himself is our peace" (Eph. 2:14). The church, called forth in Scriptures as a body of believers is unified through promise despite contrary practices. Oswald Chambers states that, "the call of God is the expression of God's nature, not man's nature; it is not about mankind's temperament, affinities or what we are best suited for. It is about the relationship between God, humanity" and each other.[6] The Bible asserts that this relationship cannot be established on one's own volition (John 6.44). Therefore, all believers are disciples of Christ, male or female, and must be empowered by God to act. The covenantal relationship with each believer entails a spiritual intervention for Scripture says: God is spirit and we relate to Him in spirit (John 4:24). It affords the revelation of God's Word that each believer is a treasure of immeasurable worth (Tit. 2:14; I Pet. 2:9). This avows the unspeakable grace bestowed on individual persons as a spiritual inheritance of a people called out from the world, saved by grace and positioned as the body of Christ. Is Christ divided? The spiritual journey of every believer should form a habitation of God through the Spirit. By the covenant relationship every believer has been transformed and transported from doom and despair to the unfathomable delight of the kingdom of God. Each individual is a component of one dynamic union, indwelt with one Spirit to assemble and act according to the purposes and assignments of God as depicted by many Scriptural accounts during the early disciple's journeys. These journeys comprised long-term and short-term assignments encompassing diverse populations; emphasizing the integral relationship of believers through covenant.

Integral through Spirit

Christian leadership has the mandate to be guided by Spiritual wisdom and discernment to command the inevitable changes inherent in any organized group of the body of Christ. Nicodemus, a religious leader by the world's standards, still lacked spiritual insight and relationship to God because he had to receive the promised Holy Spirit (John 3.7). Although he had traditional wisdom and heralded from a specialized class of individuals, Jesus questioned his ability to teach or lead the people without having Spiritual prowess (John 3. 10). Contemporary evangelical philosophy acknowledges a specialized class of individuals responsible for ministry in the church. This core of elite is not presented in the New Testament writings. "Competition and confusion created by denominational titles and sectarian labels have obscured the core vision of the gospel."[7] Paul has written that the pastor/teacher equips the saints for ministry and coaches the saints to conduct the ministry (Eph. 4:12). Modern thinking proposes that a few professionals with formal theological training carry the responsibility for the operation of God's ministry. In terms of the New Testament, the promise is that all believers, empowered by the Spirit, have their place in ministry as disciples in God's Great Commission (Mark 16:15-20). All are to build up the body of Christ in love. The interrelationship with Christ and His people imparts that the unique position of the church is the manifestation of Christ (Eph. 2:23). According to the Word of God, to forestall division in the body, differences of vocation, function or education should not avert the fact that the one ministry of Christ is shared by the whole people of God. Thus the church and the para-church are integral through the indwelling of the Holy Spirit in each member of the body of Christ. This bespeaks the biblical perspective which supports cooperation between the church and the para-church.

Integral through Purpose

The biblical requirement of the local church is to glorify God by equipping the collective of believers for the work of His ministry; "He gave some as apostles, some as prophets, some as evangelists, and some as pastors and teachers for the equipping of the saints for the work of service, to the building up of the body of Christ" (Eph. 4:11-12). The variation of roles does not subtract from the one sovereign purpose of God. Likewise titles and subtitles applied to the Church do not minimize their relationship and role in God's plan of salvation and sanctification. The integral purpose of the church and the para-church is to perform the will of God for the re-creation of the Kingdom of God. The gifts of the Holy Spirit are different and diverse, empowering individuals with tremendous ability as they proclaim the mighty acts of God mediating God's loving and reconciling work in the world. The para-church as a community of the faithful individuals and groups exemplifying Christ exhibits kindness and charity to nonbelievers as an integral component of the church. The early church's provision of food, shelter or medical care to persons injured during disagreements with Rome did not meet with disapproval from local church administrators. These servants were still recognized as Christians and members of a specific meeting location. The local church is not charged with sustaining the world but the provision of relief and support for *neighbors* in need and the people of God (Mat. 7:12: Acts 2:44-45; 4: 32-35; James 1:27). The light of compassion streams from the Holy Spirit within and is demonstrated benevolence to those outside of the communal colony of believers. In the Old Testament ecclesia benevolence is encouraged to those outside the covenant (Lev. 19: 18, 34). Although members displayed concern to individuals outside the church without the prior approval of a local church in the areas of social justice, education and health, they were not considered outcasts but remained a viable component of the life of the church. Additionally, the Holy Spirit indwells each member to signify an integral relationship. The Holy Spirit directs the church according to the purposes of God; signifying an interrelationship through purpose (John 16:13-15). According to the Word of God, once guided by the Spirit, "whoever" has been called to Spiritual beneficence is compelled to act (John 3.21). Clearly, it is incumbent to recognize that "God is not a respecter of persons and neither Jew, Greek, male or female" are anything to Him, "for we are all one in Christ," the church and the para-church, affirming God's intent for universality in His message and each comprises a respected position in Him and each other (Gal. 3.28).

Integral through Commission

The church, as a body of believers is unified as the church and the para-church through commission. The cross requires yielding, sacrifice, love and transformation. The words of Jesus to every believer is "take up your cross daily and follow me" (Luke 9:23). Through the example of Jesus we grow in faith and service. The Great Commission is a call for believers to provide the "experiential power and love of God in everyday life."[8] At the inception of Christianity, Gentiles became disciples by their experiences in the Christian community. Narrative, parable, poetry and historical facts were shared which empowered by the Holy Spirit to effect conversion. The aspect of commission which unifies each believer is it commands replication of discipleship. Discipleship is the manifestation of Christian faith. The commission binds every believer as partners in the Christian faith. Both the church and the para-church is an expression of Christian faith. The church expresses the Christian faith in its disciple-building efforts utilizing a theological language for transformation. The para-church expresses the Christian faith in its disciple-making efforts often incorporating a language "secular enough to be understood by the un-churched; perhaps using parables relative to contemporary society."[9] The goals of both institutions as disciples are identical: the transformation of lives unto God and for His glory. "Jesus left this legacy of transformational power to His disciples, who were called to continue this work."[10] We who are His disciples are the body of Christ; "each different, each crucial and each a part of one another" commissioned by the Word of God to embrace each other advocating support between the church and the para-church.[11]

Integral through Relationship

The church as a body of believers is unified through relationship. The proliferation of churches was the expectation of the early church apostles. The perspective was a communion of believers with the distinction that acceptance of salvation through Jesus Christ was all that was required. Their roles embodied organizing the disciples gathered within various assembled houses to function as a unified body with an invisible attachment to one another. Each venue was a local assembly of converts with elders, qualified by the Lord and recognized by the believers, to guide, to govern and to shepherd; and deacons who were appointed by the assembly to attend to the temporal affairs and the distribution of funds to the assembly (Acts 6:1-6; 14:23; 15:6, 23; 20:17; I Cor. 16:15; Phil. 1:1; I Thess. 5:12-13; I Tim 5:17-19). Although there is no mention of other organizations in the New Testament the numerous disciples, the unspoken expectations and the expressed commission of our Lord and Savior Jesus Christ to summon believers from the world is its indication; and if the local church was not the place for those who were not converted then the necessity for the development and proliferation of individuals, groups and organizations to obey the Great Commission becomes evident. The message of Jesus Christ is freedom of choice; His volitional proclamation is to "come, all who are the thirsty, burdened and heavy-laden" (Rev.22:17; Mt.11:28). Each disciple in relationship to one another and the world is paramount in this expression of Christ. The para-church, as the equipped saints of God is structured and outfitted to translate the message outside of the church community. It can be analogous to John the Baptist who prepared the Jewish community for Jesus; not rescinding their status as the chosen people of God but addressing impropriety and fostering relationship. The integral relationship between the church and the para-church comprises the comprehension of unity in the <u>one</u> body of Christ. Scripture incorporates the analogy of the Church, without mention of geographical location, and Jesus Christ as the embodiment of a marriage union (Eph. 5:23-32). The relationship must be based on mutual trust and respect and as each member of the body of Christ is called into this perfect union with Jesus, it becomes important that the believer contend for the durability of this relationship (Jude 3). This means:

- that similar to the natural marriage union, each member in Christ, endeavors to know and understand the will of the Father to maintain harmony and thwart disunity
- that the relationship requires communication and nurture to remain on course
- that identification and appreciation of differences eliminates pettiness and self-centeredness
- that each member of the body acknowledges all have an obligation from the Lord; and that faith and adherence to this truth will prohibit the dissolution of interconnectedness

This will enable the development of maturity and contentment implicit in Scripture as all members become united in spirit and purpose, working toward God's common goal. In spite of biblical assertions for cooperation amongst believers, there has been historical, doctrinal and practical transformation leading to factions within God's universal Church distorting and obscuring the biblical principle of unity in the body of Christ. The church and the para-church have relationship in Christ through promise. The Bible demands unity as one body of Christ admonishing an integral covenantal relationship which must diligently be preserved to enable the fulfillment of the purposes of God in the world (Eph. 4:4).

Servant Relationship

The integral relationship between the church and the para-church is a servant relationship. The servant relationship is revealed in Philippians chapter 2 which details a special type of unity in the body of Christ. It demonstrates the vulnerability of being a servant which is not necessarily compromise but submission to the will of God as each "wholeheartedly agrees with each other, loving one another and working together with one heart and purpose" (Phil. 2:2). While God's Spirit resides individually, this command applies to every Christian. Scripture demands a shared mindset; a shared philosophy with requisite humility to secure a shared process. Humility may be defined as a modest opinion or estimate of one's own importance or rank, having a proper, balanced understanding of one's own nature, sentient of both strengths and weaknesses. The Bible asserts that God, incarnate took on the form of a servant and in the face of much adversity remained committed to His purpose. The community of faithful is to be guided by this same attitude of love through service to God and one another as partners in the gospel and grace. The Word of God says: "do not merely look out for your own personal interests, but also for the interests of others" (Phil. 2:4). The church is ordered to be separate from the world because of its new nature; just as Jesus was not of this world, but to be joined to God. God effects a unity by His Spirit, mankind's nature creates conflict. The church in its entirety is ordered to concentrate on that which is befitting servanthood in Christ Jesus.

A servant relationship in Christ entails the Holy Spirit's guidance since mankind cannot emulate Christ or know the mind of Christ of his own volition. However, The Bible suggests that believers are made anew and have the mind of Christ through the Holy Spirit and do not have the same perspective as the world which is one of division, jealousy, arrogance, pride, covetousness and revelry (II Cor. 5:16-17). The Word of God says: "not by might, nor by power, but by My Spirit," and "I will put My Spirit within you" (Eze. 36:27; Zech. 4:6). The Holy Spirit of God reigns in the body of believers to afford complete connection and interdependence as each member is employed as God's servant and servant to each other.

The servant relationship represents surrender. The church and the para-church, both undeniably members of one body through Christ, are admonished to die to self and to live for Christ (Gal.2:20). Paul urges that every believer remember that the ultimate surrender was Jesus dying the death of the cross (Phil. 2: 8). He presents Jesus' free surrender of His divine authority to take the status of a lowly servant to obtain victory for God. Although He had the sovereign authority over humanity, He accepted becoming a slave to it; sharing in the detriment of mankind for its betterment. "He acted as one who was obedient rather than as one who called for obedience to Himself."[12] He concealed His Divinity, beneath mortal flesh and became the bond-servant of God and mankind. By this, Christ encourages the same subjection by the heirs to the kingdom, the individual members that comprise the church, in their relationship between God and each other. Believers are required to participate together in God's redemptive work with integrity, giving primacy to the brethren, in so doing we are blessed and Jesus is exalted to the glory of God the Father (Phil 2:14-18; James 1:25). The Bible expresses the necessity of mutual accord in the purposes of God revealed by the servant relationship required of every Christian as support for cooperation between the church and the para-church.

Integral through Responsibility

Jesus, who did not despise His role in the purposes of God and managed His task with diligence and fervor, is an example that necessitates adherence to the responsibilities of each member of the family of God. Discipleship, spiritual growth and maturity are the responsibility of the church. The church as the assembled believers "is not to create demand for religious experience but rather to address and effectively satisfy the demand that exists."[13] According to *World Christian Trends* at the heart of church vitality which appropriated the widespread movement of Christianity "were its internal waves of renewal which were effective both in renewing peoples already Christian and in the extension of the gospel to people not yet Christian."[14] The church is to build up God's elect for works of service which are needed inside and outside of the walls of the church. "Christianity is meant to function in society as a creative force in the culture."[15] Categorically, the mandate for the Church is *"Receive! Go! Witness! Proclaim! Disciple! Baptize! Train!"*[16] This is the integral responsibility of the church and the para-church. In Scripture, the church is acknowledged as the primary arena for discipleship of believers. This formed assembly "devoted themselves to the apostle's teaching and fellowship, to the breaking of bread and the prayers" (Acts 2:42). The Word of God insists that this community *meet* and is commanded to "stir up one another to love and good works" (Heb. 10:24-25). Guided by the

Holy Spirit, the servant relationship is affirmed as each member ordained, designed and uniquely gifted for God's purpose is decidedly linked together through creation and promise. Scripture depicts the integral relationship between the church and the para-church affirming that one sacrifice is sufficient for all, "for by one offering God has perfected for all time those who are sanctified;" and having "a great priest over the house of God," every believer can "draw near with a sincere heart in confidence" (Heb. 10:14, 21-22). Review of literature indicates the perspective that the para-church should be positively appreciated as "helpers, raised up by God to aid the church, but possessing a status subordinate to that of the church."[17] This is not intended in Scripture which asserts that the church is "not adequate in itself, but its adequacy is from God" (II Cor. 3:6). The claim of theological priority for the church considered a distinct entity, rather than an organism or communal colony of believers which has one unified purpose distinguishable by assignment and gifting, is unscriptural. The Bible says:

> God has allotted to *each* a measure of faith. So we who are many are *one body* in Christ and *individually* members of one another. And since we have gifts that differ according to the grace given to us, let each exercise them accordingly (Rom. 12:4-6).

Each believer has entered into a viable covenantal and servant relationship with the Most High God and with every believer. Each has as its responsibility the mandate to value, appreciate and love each other. When the church loses sight of its responsibility being inundated with fragmentation and monolithic perspectives it besmirches the cause of Jesus Christ. Scripture affirms that "a house divided will not stand," therefore congregational members are to be engaged and not repudiated by being placed on the periphery (Mat.12:25; Mark 3:25; Luke 11:17). Every member of the body of Christ has the responsibility to live as disciples to God.

Integral through Partnership as Children of God

The servant relationship conveyed in Scripture assumes partnership amongst the children of God. The church and the para-church are integral in nature, history and in the universal presence of Christ. Both affirm the kerygma as its essence, the work of the Holy Spirit and each have a pivotal role in the overall mission of the universal Church. Predicated upon the servant relationship between Christians and the church and para-church in particular, the far-reaching goal of the para-church is to direct new converts to the local church whereby spiritual development can be accomplished. In Scripture, the activities of groups or individuals which correspond to a para-church were the bands of disciples and individuals who journeyed through the lands as representatives or ambassadors, teaching and preaching the gospel. As biblically affirmed children of God, their mission included church planting, member edification and conversion (I Cor. 3: 6-9). These participants in the restoration of the kingdom of God were in a servant relationship with God and other believers, often identified as the church, assisting with church implementation and spiritual development. Peter was a servant of Christ and believers, though he was the foundational message bearer for the Christian community to establish the church (Mat. 16:18). Disseminating the message of the gospel was the tool to institute the church. The gospel is the foundation of the church; the church is not the foundation of the gospel. The universal Church, functions by implementing innovative methods suitable to particular context and "lack of contact between Christians and non-Christians may be viewed in the context of society's great social problems."[18] The ideal perspective of the church has been to engage in activities with neighboring congregations to recapture the kind of cooperative spirit affirmed by the early New Testament church. "The hoped for union" of churches as the body of Christ, "has become instead one of schisms and lack of cooperation."[19] Alternatively, the para-church organization "with its own independently-stated plans" seeks recognition as an ally to form strategic partnerships with the church.[20] The evangelistic efforts of the para-church involve addressing societal need, building relationship through various medium and disseminating the Word of God oftentimes by methods not available to the church.

Augustine's narrative "regarding the origin, history and deserved ends of two cities; the earthly and heavenly cities which are in the world commingled and implicated with one another," exposes the complexities of the local church and the para-church.[21] The philosophical tenets and ideology of Scripture is the admonishment that all of mankind preserve unity through partnership as children of God. "Since the mind of humanity, though naturally capable of reason and intellect, is disabled by besetting and inveterate vices," often unwittingly dissonance becomes normative.[22] In the absence of a servant relationship to bind the two parallels, the para-church finds itself in conceptual exile in the secular world apart from the local church and categorized as a refugee by the church.[23] Like the dialectic tale of *Two Cities*, the natural perspective of life presents opposing views which leads to obstruction, division, separation and compartmentalizing; distancing believers from God and each other. Historically, human society and cultures have been riddled with barriers such as assigned classes: slave, free, rich, poor, Jew and Gentile. Christ eliminated distinctions (Col.3:11). The biblical pronouncement of partnership expressed as members of one body supports cooperation between the church and the para-church.

Chapter Summary

Current trends defines para-church as almost church, partly church; a service of the church offering alternate or revival worship unrelated to an existing church.[24] This perspective ignites the controversy and necessitates identifiers specific to a religious organization which does not represent itself as a church or alternate but an apostolate. An organization of the laity devoted to the mission of the Church; an association of individuals for the dissemination of a religion or doctrine; distinct and separate. The term apostolate "finds expression through the missionary vision" of the Great Commission to disunite the church and the para-church as the universal congregation.[25] "Like Saints Peter and Paul, as apostles to the un-churched, unbelieving and uncertain, clerical authority should serve as administrators, teachers, advisors and pastors who inspire and coordinate the disciple-making efforts of laity."[26] Every member of the body of Christ is interrelated in a covenantal and servant relationship of submission to God and each other. The covenantal relationship precipitates unification between God and humanity. The Servant relationship characterizes the love between God and humanity finding expression relative to mankind. Each relationship is more about a spirit of concern for the intentions of God and less about hierarchical arrangements. The reciprocity inferred by this relationship conveys mutual consideration, self-denial, yielding and love to promote orderliness and edification. Enmeshed in this conceptual framework is the biblical truth that every believer will give an account of themselves in service to Christ and the Lord will judge the decisions made; including those concerning conscience (Rom. 14:12; I Cor. 3:11-15). The Bible informs that individual salvation is through faith and "no flesh will be justified by works of the law" (Gal. 2:16). As the Church of one body in unity with Christ, each member has the choice to build upon a foundation of "gold, silver and precious gems" displaying good works in Christ's name, of obedience, mercy and dedicated service to glorify God; or to build upon a foundation of "wood, stubble and hay" exhibited as defiance, superficial behaviors and selfish motives without spiritual value (I Cor. 3:13-15). Accordingly, each believer will be judged and rewarded predicated upon obedience, mercy, faith and service which are suggestive of position in Christ, who is head of the Church (Mat.7:20; 16: 27; John 13:34-35; Rev. 20:13).

The Book of Philemon narrates the integrality of believers regardless of station through the introduction of Onesimus, a runaway slave, repositioned as a free man in Christ Jesus. His faith and acceptance as a child of God warrants treatment as a brother. Despite his natural state being a submissive position, he was to be regarded as equal to Paul, Philemon's friend and fellow believer. Herein lies the message of Christ to the church regarding the para-church: that Jesus' death was the final covenant and expression of servant relationship for the whole body of believers destroying any partition that separates children of God from the Father and one another; and His resurrection provides the propitiation for acceptance as an heir to the eternal covenant encompassing an integral relationship between believers. The biblical support of cooperation between the church and the para-church is in the assertion that every being that acknowledges Jesus in the flesh is a child of God, is established by covenant in relationship with God, is sufficient in Him, in partnership with other believers; integral through servanthood and individually responsible to God alone (John 14:4).

Is Christ divided? The Spirit of God attests to the integrality of every believer in Christ (Rom. 8:16-17). Although the para-church may be required by human sensibilities to present as subordinate to the church this concept lacks a biblical basis as determined by Scriptural focus on impartiality and is illustrative of Jesus' assertion that "no prophet is welcome in his hometown" (Luke 14:24). The Bible says that no man should esteem themselves; exhorting even those in authority to take the low seat until invited to advance (Luke 14: 8-11; Rom. 12:3). "The biblical teaching on submission focuses primarily on the spirit with which we view other people and does not purposively set forth a series of hierarchical relationships."[27] Its intent is to communicate an inner attitude of mutuality. Scripturally, in a reciprocal servant relationship the para-church is not represented as a subordinate to the church and neither is the para-church to exaggerate its identity (Rom. 12:3). Servant relationship is voluntary submission and an obligatory posture for all Christians. The integrality between the church and the para-church is represented by the covenant and servant relationship, touted by Scripture and is the biblical foundation for conciliation and support between them.

CHAPTER 6

MALFUNCTIONING OF ONE PART IMPLICATES ANOTHER PART

According to contemporary standards the determination of healthy, thriving, growing faith communities is exhibited by characteristics that can be identified, measured and maximized using scientific methods of worldly organizations noted as empirical measures instituted within a metaphysical realm. Data collected regarding church attendance and finance constitutes the elements of a successful church. However, the Bible proposes that an essential component of the local church is engagement of individual members in a bond of community. Instituting the engagement of all members within the faith community enables increased spiritual commitment, satisfaction and support. It allows the utilization of spiritual gifts, talents and motivations in the work of the church which is assigned by God. Often the constituency is in touch with its surrounding "community having awareness of environmental changes such as a variance in the ethnic and cultural composition of the neighborhood and decline in theological distinctiveness."[1] Without the engagement of its congregants, the church can "become community-unfriendly commuter congregations with an out-of-touch membership" and ineffective ministry.[2] The para-church, comprising church members, becomes an effective conduit between the church and the community with its focus on embracing Christian values, social concerns and instituting evangelism as practice through lifestyle. The para-church has as its literal expressed interest outreach toward the lost. The existence of the church and the para-church necessitate the development of coalitions as both are components of the universal Church representing locally the Great Commission of God. Church leadership must find precedence in the Scriptural intention that every believer forms the basis of the local church and every believer is an appendage of the body of Christ conveying the universality and totality of God. The church must "stimulate an internal spiritual renaissance within their walls" and advocate a "growth-stimulating interdependence" with the para-church.[3] The revelation of God's word is that every believer is of immeasurable worth and coexists in Christ (Titus 2:4; I Pet. 2:9). This interrelationship imparts that the church and the para-church have a unique capacity, each comprising individuals called out from the world, saved by grace and privileged to be positioned in the body of Christ as heirs with specific assignment. The spiritual journey of every believer forms an environment of God and therefore should afford a bond of community. Is Christ divided? The biblical assertion that each member, individually and collectively are indwelt with One Spirit supports cooperation between the church and the para-church establishing one dynamic union to act according to the plan of God.

The Universality and Totality of God

The Bible attests to the universality and totality of God. God dispatched a sacrifice; His Son, to atone for humanity's choice of separation from Him (John 3:16). The ontological perspective of God presumes a Creator with no beginning and no ending; one who is an all-encompassing complete being. Consequently, individuals must be drawn to Him in order to know Him and following transformation will exist for Him.

Scriptures literate that even under chastisement, the natural tendency of man is to profane God and sin willfully, wickedly, and arrogantly. Therefore, God offers his mercy to the world and ingratiates every believer with the gift of grace that would never occur based upon merit. Each presentation and attainment of grace is representative the universality and totality of God. It is also personal and individual negating self indulgence and presumptuousness. An example of a Christian serving in leadership, Paul wrote that though he could boast about his authoritative position and acknowledge confidence in his human accomplishments toward his role in leadership, the only important aspect in life, of which he exhorts disciples "to follow his example," is being granted the ability to stand before God on the basis of faith alone and being a disciple of Christ (Phil. 3:4-11). A search of the Word of God reveals the Creator's intent that all of mankind establishes an allegiance with Him through the final covenant in Christ.

Jesus is demonstrated as the ultimate leader through many examples of performing God's bidding. The universality and totality of God resonates in His quest that no one should perish. This conceptual framework is the summation of leadership as empowerment. It is noteworthy that He engaged the disciples as participants, commissioned them to "go" everywhere and they were dispersed throughout every locale but conjoined in Him. By design it is necessary that every believer as members of the body of Christ engage in the work of the Lord. Cleansed, each is to be a vessel of honor, sanctified, useful to the Master, and prepared for every good work (II Tim 3:21). The Bible affirms that there are many members of one body in Christ, each is individually members of one another and God creates every Christian to "use gifts and talents in ministry" in the church and in the world (Mark 10:45; Rom. 12:5 Col. 3:23-24; James 1:22).[4]

According to Warren, "most people associate the term membership with paying dues, meaningless ritual, silly rules, handshakes and having your name on some dusty roll," which may be attributed to church leadership who oppose involvement with other Christians with a different address.[5] Christian leadership should regard that the Christianity of the Bible asserts that all believers have had the status of stranger to God and foreigner to heaven removed to become members of God's family belonging to God's household with every other Christian (Eph. 2:19). It becomes imperative to the mission of Kingdom building to view every believer as a child of God with direct Spiritual interface. The request of leaders is to "test the Spirit," not ignore them as having little value (I John 4:1). Leaders are obliged to determine the commission of every believer utilizing the biblical criteria of integrity of character, soundness of doctrine and Spiritual capacity (Mat.7:15-20; Luke 24:46-47; Gal. 5:22-26; I Tim. 3:1-13-17; 4:3-6; 6:3-4; II Tim. 2:15; Tit. 1:5-11; James 3: 17-18). The church attempts to invalidate the para-church based on context, traditions, prejudice and possible misunderstandings. The Bible affirms that unity of the body of Christ can only be obtained by removing obstacles through teaching, sufficient understanding and adherence of every believer to the totality and universality of God and the revealed Truth in His Word.

All are Disciples in a Divine Purpose

To effectively engage church membership requires leadership with the supernatural perspective designed by the Holy Spirit, expressed in God's Word for His glory. Traditional ideologies of leadership endorse constraints on the positions and functions of various constituencies in the church and the para-church. As Leith Anderson asserts, "leadership and celebrity rarely mix well. To be a celebrity is to have a status above others, to be elevated and honored in ways not available to almost everyone else," which often "causes a person to think more highly of himself than he ought to think."[6] Luke 6: 40 states: "a disciple is not above his teacher, but everyone when he is fully trained will be like his teacher." The contention is that some church leaders dismantle the abilities and inhibit the enthusiasm of its membership by advocating "loyalties" to limiting cultural traditions which impair spiritual growth. "When churches refocus on the core Christian traditions, the transforming power of the gospel becomes unfettered."[7] The need of every believer is to become a mature Christian, enabled to function in service to God according to the purpose of their existence. The Word of God states that the Christian is to be one who listens and heeds the commandments, precepts and aims of God to become "an effectual doer; for how can they hear without a preacher" (Jam. 1:22; Rom. 10:14). "When any Christian's schedule consists completely of receiving biblical input with no outflow of ministry or evangelism, spiritual growth will stagnate."[8] The para-church, comprising members of the church, are Christians who, often without the tutelage of church leadership, can be observed as persons who accept the call to discipleship and "assume responsibility through personal sacrifice to turn promising ideas into action."[9] Since the beginning, after the fall of the first man, Adam, the divine "purpose of God has been for the believer to be like His Son."[10] Even the relationship of discipleship is choreographed by God, since believers in the Lord Jesus Christ must have the Spirit of God otherwise that believer is none of His (Rom. 8: 9). The connotation is that the teaching and pastoring comprising the local church is orchestrated by God, but the operative is the Spirit which causes the believer to "walk in the statutes, keep God's judgments and do them" (Eze.36:26-27). Therefore, leadership should consider the honor of their positions and execute them graciously as servants of God.

The Holy Spirit of God enlightens every believer presenting with clarity the truths in God's Word and by the Holy Spirit the believer develops into Christ's disciple. An individual's obedience profits spiritual growth and maturity affording the transformation of human character to the requisite Christ-like character of the Bible. Leadership entails development, empowerment and accountability and equipping the saints of God consists of developing them into mature disciples, preparing them for personal ministry and enabling them to fulfill their life mission as disciples of Christ in service for God. Consequently, it is essential that leadership avert the conflict and competition that exists between the believers constituting the church and the para-church. Scripture mandates unity within the body of Christ and the avoidance of forming opinions that although may be logical are not Spiritual. The chosen people of God, the Israelites of the Old Testament, wrongly assumed that the altar built by their brethren was a sign of rebellion against God (Josh. 22:9-34). They prepared for war against their own relatives. Leaders of the children of Israel were dispatched to discuss the ensuing treachery and through candid discussion determined that the purpose for the altar was to be a witness to God as the sovereign Lord of all the elect for every generation (Josh. 22: 24-29). The challenge for the local church is to reexamine its constructs and effectiveness in the areas acknowledged by the Scriptures and consider its efficiency in the areas addressed by the para-church, accepting that fundamentally, members of a congregation of believers have the need to respond to the command of the Spirit. Jesus, the Christ, had one purpose while on earth: "to draw all men" unto Himself (John 12:32). The cross was His method. Is Christ divided? Being disciples of Christ, each have a specified mission and method, therefore, the local church and the para-church should recognize the various roles, participation and contributions of both institutions.

All are Empowered for a Divine Purpose

Before we can effectively *make disciples* of the nations, we must learn to be disciples. Since the church is a body; all parts have functions and are to be set in motion to accomplish unique and unified tasks. Evangelism is central to leadership but not exclusive; therefore, an effective leader must acknowledge that they too are a disciple. The administrative leadership within the church must not function as rulers but promote empowerment. Jesus stated that all authority in heaven and on earth belongs to Him; and reminded the apostles that they were His disciples (Mat.28:18). The apostles were the Christian leaders who established the early church. They were the example of discipleship for the new converts. They preached, instructed, planted new churches, performed baptism and evangelized. All that was done was to advance the divine purpose of God for His glory. Paul admonishes Timothy to develop many leaders stating: "the things you have heard from me in the presence of many witnesses, these commit to faithful men, who will be able to teach others also" (II Tim. 2:2). Leaders, and disciples are to be reproduced so that the church may grow and mature; and each is to operate within their giftedness according to the calling and authority of God. In the church, equipping is usually accomplished through the preaching of the pastor, ministerial teaching staff and lay teachers. The command of the Bible for the church urges the task of reproducing disciples "in all nations"that the divine purpose of God will go forth and "no one should perish" (Mat. 28:19; I Tim. 2:4; Pet. 3:9). This statement in effect supports the rationale that the ministry within the local church must mobilize the members to maturity in Christ in preparation to serve outside of the local church in the community implicating the biblical perspective supports cooperation between the church and the para-church.

Apostles, evangelists, prophets, pastors and teachers are characteristic of the leadership which have been provided by God to educate and empower the church to attain the desired results (Eph. 4:11-12). Christian administrators have a responsibility to recognize the various gifts within the congregation or para-church. The spiritual gifts of the saints are often discovered through prayer and in the context of communal involvement, leadership interaction and discipleship training. It is imperative that leadership encourage its members to utilize spiritual gifts for the edification of the church and to complement one another to good works that are both inside and outside of the local church (I Cor. 12: 12-27). The Lord said to Isaiah, "It is too small a thing that you should be my servant to raise up the tribes of Jacob, and to restore the preserved ones of Israel; I will also make you a light of the nations so that my salvation may reach to the end of the earth"(Is. 49:6). Jesus is that light that came into the world and required that all who believe take up their cross, follow Him and also become fishers of men (Mat. 4:19; Luke 9:23; John 8:12). The greatest motivation for the para-church is biblical. As children of God the para-church must walk in obedience to the biblical mandate to fulfill the Great Commission. Following this perspective the para-church operates under guidelines that incorporate *strategically* what God requires. It is necessary for the local church to prepare disciples to be fishers of men, who in turn will be the example of a disciple by the life that they lead; having the impact of restoring communities and translating new disciples into the local church where the process of spiritual maturity is conveyed and disciples are empowered for divine purpose.

All are Designed for Divine Purpose

There is a connection between a divine commission to an assignment and the delegation to perform the assignment. A divine commission entails an acknowledged acceptance of responsibility and the divine enablement to see the task through to fruition. God's delegation of authority by His grace, equips each citizen of the Kingdom to use gifts received to serve one another and to faithfully administer God's love (I Pet. 4:10). The Scriptural reality is that every person exists according to the plan of the Master Creator. The para-church composed of Christian believers has a specialized ministry and exists as an integral portion of God's plan. An adequate balance must be attained between the responsibilities of the church and the para-church to enable the scripturally required establishment of His Kingdom. The contention that the para-church is illegitimate or analogous to the church ignores the principle of human beings being singly members of the church. Individuals involved in the para-church take their mission seriously. They are grounded in accountability and faithfulness to the Word of God which demonstrates legitimacy, significance and compulsory contribution to the Kingdom of God. The members of the church who engage in ministry as the para-church express amazement and disillusionment regarding the unacceptance by the church. Demonstrably and Scripturally the Body of Christ, the para-church declares right standing and Christ's authority. Some church leaders discourage and even rebuke anyone who endorses a local para-church in reference to providing human, financial, material and capital resources. The ability to share resources becomes more palatable with the acceptance of the biblical truth that everything belongs to God. Any concerns the church has regarding jurisdiction and the para-church is discounted by the biblical accounts or mandate of God that every believer is to participate in His mission of Kingdom building. The same Source that sanctions the church sanctions the speciously labeled para-church. The biblical perspective supports cooperation between the church and the para-church as reflected by the fulfillment of Jesus' promise in the New Testament whereby the Holy Spirit anoints all of God's people for works of service and ministry; assenting that it is God who anoints, seals for His ownership, places His Spirit within and causes each individual to stand firm in Christ (Acts 2:17,38; Rom. 12:6-8; I Cor. 12:4-11; II Cor. 1:22; I Thess. 4:8; I Pet. 2:5; Rev. 1:6).

The church designed as the place of nurture for the body of Christ is admonished to limit exchange and fellowship with unbelievers though all are required to witness of God (II Cor. 6:14-15). The para-church is the witnessing sector, still the function of the church, instituted individually or as groups, designed for divine purpose. Blackaby and King assert that "because the church is the body of Christ," *alive and active,* "it functions best when all members are able to share what they sense God wants the church to be and to do."[11] The Bible attests that the context of Christianity presupposes a "common salvation" which should be established as a correspondence in mission between all believers, in this instance, the church and the para-church (Jude 1:3).

The Local church and the Para-church have Specified Mission

Scripture states that every believer is under a microscope; and therefore should live wisely, gain spiritual knowledge to communicate God's message successfully in life and speech; and the Christian witness should be palatable for effectiveness (II Cor. 3:2; Col. 4:5-6). Fitch asserts that the local church is instituted toward the building of the Body of Christ and the sanctification of believers "through instruction which advocates evangelism, witness and growth."[12] Therefore, one of the roles and responsibilities of the local church is to prepare its membership for the aforementioned tasks. The para-church seeks to elicit a link between the church which is limited by geographical locations, and the outside world by extending the reach of the church as a viable expression of the body of Christ. However, it is perceived as giving away ownership of evangelism to "para-church organizations and expert techniques and, in the process, making the church a sideshow."[13] When considering the options of ministry that the para-church chooses from the many and varied opportunities that exist in our capitalistic or religiously homogenized society, perhaps as with every institution referred to man, without proper safeguards, the capacity for illegitimacy, greed and fraud exits. In these instances the church has the responsibility of instruction in accountability and engaging the leadership of each institution as co-laborers together, sharing resources for the common cause of Christ and contributing to the guidance of Christian discipleship through "advice, encouragement and work" as assignment.[14] The para-church, as members of the body of Christ, aligns itself with the gospel message and biblical principles to assure the demonstration of alliance with Jesus' mission and commitment. "It is necessary to address the controversy of separation, dissonance, and avoidance that exists between the para-church and the local church to elicit an efficacious relationship enabling the advancement of the existing and eventual Kingdom of God upheld in the truths of God's Word. Doctrinal controversy, denominationalism and separation afford parochialism which diminishes societal outreach. Concurrently, the secularization and plurality of society places many individuals outside of the influence of the local or traditional church and the observed discord prohibits positive transactions.

Each institution has been given specified mission in the divine plan of God. The church has been established to be the primary arena of discipleship for believers. Following acceptance of the gospel, the formulation of community became a necessary aspect of Christianity. New believers "devoted themselves to the apostles' teaching and fellowship, to the breaking of bread and prayers" (Acts2:42). The continuation of assembly was insisted as Scripture advocates local fellowship in order "to stir up one another to love and good works" (Heb. 10:24-25). Christian administrators were admonished to edify believers in preparation for life as the church body and every church regardless of locale observed the ordinances; inclusive of baptizing new Christians (Eph. 4:12; I Thes. 5:11; Tim. 1-13). The para-church was represented by apostles who traveled disseminating the gospel in varied places. Their mission included church planting, edification of church membership and evangelism to the un-churched (Acts 8: 35-37; I Cor. 3:6, 9). Is Christ divided? The specified mission of church members labeled the para-church is assistance in its communal propensity and progression. The local church is the nucleus of the community of faithful and its specified mission is fusion of the body of Christ to effect the kingdom of God; the melding together of the individual parts into one whole. According to *World Christian Trends*, technology is becoming the determinant of how the church and the world interacts, even providing "surrogacy" that is a threat to replace God as the object of worship.[15] Spiritual development is a process which unfolds through instruction that supports disciplined effort. It is individualized, but does not progress in the absence of others (Prov. 27:17; Rom.15: 14). The para-church, often comprised of trained church members, as the evangelistic and discipleship component of the church offers the aspect of relationship that God requires (I Cor. 13). A mistaken perception of the para-church ensues when church leadership defines them as "visionaries who discern what they believe to be a need" instead of defining them as members of the body of Christ endeavoring for the Great Commission of Christ.[16] For the para-church, the Great Commission is a requirement that believers provide the experiential power and love of God (Luke 24:45-46). The biblical perspective which supports cooperation between the church and the para-church is its affirmation of the specialized role and responsibility of every believer in the divine purpose of God (Jer.1:4-5; Acts 17:28; Eph.1:11).

God has set the Agenda

The church has a rich cultural heritage. Christianity is a religion and a culture. Cultural heritage embodies history, tradition and purposive long-term action. It encompasses acknowledged, cohesive practical policies with which generations of people establish bonds of fellowship and reciprocity. The early church era expounded upon the principles of Christ as the Passover Lamb much in the way of Israel's Passover Feast. As the church, it is imperative to commemorate this time of redemption resolutely, explicating truths, promoting sound doctrine, training in righteousness expressed as charitable acts. God has set the agenda of the church as an institution built by God in Christ. Its founder and chief administrator is Jesus Christ who died to save all who believe encompassing the universal Church. Christ being the authority and foundation of the universal Church establishes that the local church is the body of Christ. It is everlasting and is called the bride of Christ. Christ accomplishes the edifying of His bride, through ordained and gifted servants who, through the Holy Spirit, are placed in the roles of perfecting believers, disciples of Christ, for the work of ministry for which each have been Spiritually gifted to perform. The para-church, like the church, has Divine commission to an assignment and delegated membership to perform the assignment. It is described as having "a clear *Christian identity* and purpose yet," due to the absence of "ties to a particular congregation or denomination," it is banned and disfranchised as the functioning members of the body of Christ.[17] The Bible elicits an institution of people who are bound by a common faith; universally and collectively empowered to act by the Holy Spirit. God has set the agenda.

Mankind has defined the limitations of the biblical church. From a humanistic point of view, individual perspectives regarding the church and the para-church vary according to position and involvement; often these perspectives produce tolerance or opposition. However, God has set the agenda. The Scripturally-specified role of the church is one of "equipping of the saints for the works of service" (Ep. 4.12). There is no specified outreach movement for the pastorate office, other than toward the children of God who are identified as sinners saved by grace (Eph. 2:8). According to Scripture, to overcome intolerance, disunity and opposition we are to "preserve the unity of the Spirit in the bond of peace; having one God and Father of all who is over all and through all and in all; having given to each one of us a measure of faith and grace; for we are members of one another" (Rom. 12.3; Ep. 4.3, 6, 7, 25). The local church as an institution of God must be mindful, when embarking on activities that are not specified as the responsibilities of the local church body, not to conform itself to the secular culture surrounding it. Conformity to the secular culture is seen as compromise and effects change in purpose which is the spiritual growth of the saints. Rick Warren states that the local church should not be "driven by the needs of unbelievers."[18] Truly it is not a question that the local church comprises sinners, however, the determined composition is that of believers and others of inquiry (Acts 2). Benevolence, social and political processes and participation may be observed as taking too much of the local church's attention; taking the focus away from equipping, supporting, admonishing, and shepherding causing division and sects. By divine appointment "the church has a higher calling" rather than to allow its agenda be determined by the masses.[19]

Since God has set the agenda there is an expectancy of comfort in the congregation because the institution is made up of individuals having the same faith. As each member's subjugated soul is presented before the throne of a perfect, holy and just God; accepting the merciful release of His forgiveness through the blood of Jesus Christ, there is an environment of consolation in the congregation. A church driven by the purposes of God will maintain this perspective by focusing on its biblical foundation (I Cor. 3:10-11). Christian leadership has the Spirit-endowed ability and divine assignment to ascertain the correct purpose, goals and objectives of the group, and to develop the necessary structure and plan to lead people to accomplish their purpose. Jesus, as our administrator demonstrated a willingness to take responsible risks to bring prominence to the directive as evidenced by His death. According to Charles Tidwell, effective administration of the local church "is the guidance provided by church leaders as they lead the church to use its spiritual, human, physical, and financial resources to move the church toward reaching its objectives and fulfilling its avowed purposes."[20] It is enabling the children of God who comprise the church to become and to do, by God's grace. The church and the para-church are part of a corporate body of believers. The Bible attests that every believer is the Church and as such must rely on the counsel of God through the Word of God, universal prayer and other believers. God has set the agenda contending that believers do not stand alone. The attestation of the word of God avows unity, fellowship, and accountability one to the other. Accordingly, God, who has set the agenda, has created the church to represent Him to the world as a thriving organization of the faithful, who regardless of denomination, church affiliation, association or para-church is mutually interdependent through His Spirit.

Gifts and Talents given for God's Agenda

The church represents the visible earthly conglomeration of believers. It is an assembly of the body of believers to be a supernatural reconstruction of the Spiritual capacities of Jesus Christ. Jesus demonstrated the unconditional, unrequited love of God for all creation and insists that acknowledgement would be the same love demonstrated to each other (I John 4:20). This is impossible by natural means therefore mankind's natural talents, abilities, mental capacities and emotions are supernaturally imbued by the Holy Spirit to be utilized for God's purpose. As Scripture states, the Spirit exists and moves about as the wind, going where it wills, coming from a place that cannot be discerned and which cannot be observed. It cannot be contained, but is sent by God to comfort, guide and intercede. The giving of the Spirit to every believer has distinction in resolve, utility and effect for God's agenda. The equipping, preparation and edification of believers involves development of the gifts to benefit the body of Christ. Spiritual gifts are manifested to enable the body of believers to function as a unit affording administrative capabilities, leadership and effective operations. Every child of God has innate abilities for teaching, serving, leading, giving and encouraging with varying efficacy according to the measure attributed by God to each individual. For example, Scripture states "all have been given a measure of faith" (Rom. 12:3). This measure could mean belief in the midst of circumstances or it could mean a supernatural confidence in God. Scripture asserts that every believer, having a measure of faith, is mandated to share the message of the gospel. Although, having the spiritual gift of evangelism assures that through faith, while sharing the gospel the believer will be able to achieve connection with others for Christ. This concept reaffirms that Spiritual gifts are given as a means to perform the tasks assigned in God's agenda. The Bible contends that *God requires order* indicating that each individual's gift brings unity and stability to the local and universal body. The biblical assertion is this can only be accomplished if "we love God with all of our heart, soul, mind, and strength and love one another as we love ourselves" (Mat. 22:37-39; Mark 12:30-31).

Believers, individually and collectively, are commanded to witness of God. The believers' witness of the validity of Christ is predicated upon the Holy Spirit. Jesus as an example, following His baptism received the Holy Spirit then began His earthly ministry performing miracles, healings, demonstrations of faith, prophesying, discerning spirits and most importantly, communicating with the Father. Scripture attests that all of Jesus' activities were a sign for believers and unbelievers. The biblical records claim is that the body of believers remain on earth to validate Christ as authentic and God as relational. Each member has the gifts to testify, glorify and minister according to God's agenda as the need arises. Paul demonstrated this by his missionary journeys and explication that whatever the circumstances he would persist in the tasks assigned him by the Lord, satisfied with the provisions of God (Phil.4:11-13). Every believer is accountable to God being "called according to His purpose" (Rom. 8: 28). It is only with the inclusion and exercise of each individual member, functioning together and utilizing gifts according to God's agenda that Christians can mature and evolve into the future Kingdom of God.

Christian leadership is obliged to be mindful that the purpose, mission and prerogative of the church can only be accomplished in accordance with the commands of Scripture. The intricacy of the body of Christ indicates that the aim of Christian leadership should be to assure that all parts are in operation, functioning appropriately and in conjunction with the will of God. The machinations of mankind endeavor to place limits, rules, regulations and stipulations contrary to the unification espoused in Scripture. The Bible states that if believers "have died to the elementary principles of the world they do not submit to decrees in accordance with the commandments and teachings of men" (Col. 2:20-22). The perception held by Christian leaders regarding the para-church is dividing the body of Christ. The divisiveness apparent through diminished support, lack of parishioner engagement and a territorial stance creates dwindling church membership, ineffectual ministry and non-Christian influence. When there is universal acceptance by church leadership of Spiritual gifting through the Holy Spirit of each believer with consequential appointments for witness in God's agenda, comprehension may lead to cooperation; and cooperation may alleviate tension between the church and the para-church

Dr. Felecia Rodgers

facilitating unity against contradictions to the biblical assertions of one body, one God, and one Spirit.

THE CHARACTER OF DENOMINATIONALISM

Early church history describes the first century church as infused with the determination to spread the gospel of Jesus Christ. The church developed and proliferated by evangelism. The mission-minded members of the various house churches were impelled to take the life they shared within the congregation to the hostile outside world.[21] The insurgence of multiple ecclesiologies ushered in denominations with new perspectives for the church. According to Payne, as new sects were created, the church exchanged its focus from being mission-minded to a maintenance-minded model resulting in a significant decline in church membership as evangelism and outreach to the community was truncated and the church was constrained to address social issues.[22] Denominationalism has been in existence in some form even before the Reformation. Paul asserts that while imprisoned "fellow workers for the kingdom of God, who are of the circumcision have proved to be a comfort to me," portraying an aspect of identity that may be expressed as denominationalism among believers (Col 4:11). It is predicated upon divisive philosophical and theological perspectives between Christians that caused separation and necessitated the establishment of institutions that have been described as Christian churches with minimally cooperative endeavors having degrees of affiliation and varied hierarchal forms of government. "A church denomination may be defined as a group of Christians that have their own interpretation of aspects of Christian theology and their own organization."[23] The local church is the central expression and educator for evangelism and discipleship. It is where members are *reared* for service and submission. Denominationalism denotes the diverse character of the congregation and is not inherently bad. It exhibits much traditionalism and ritualism that has its place in religious practices often incorporated as methods of identification and cohesion, the value and necessity of which affords a substantial intrinsic relationship that is espoused in Scripture. Characteristically invasive procedures validated by the local church enamor the believer and the visitor as efforts of enlightenment to eliminate obscurity through preaching, praising, worshiping, established ordinances and prayer to bring attention to the Source of light. Such is the task of the body of believers as the para-church participating in the work of evangelism and discipleship without the consequence of denominationalism, to those outside of the church. Dissuading compromise to the mission, message and methods of the local church, the para-church constructs societal changes by allowing the Holy Spirit's light to shine from within before mankind in such a way that every believer's good works may be seen by the unbelieving world and these works attributed to God, the one authority; our Heavenly Father (Matt. 5:13-15).

It is necessary for the church to be an expression of the realities of God and a genuine manifestation of God's intent. Regardless of denomination, Christianity must be concerned with fostering life-changing relationship in Christ. The contemporary church's emphasis on separate identity rather than on Christ, denominational Christianity and a lack of personal accountability through love and relationship appears much like the varied sects of Jesus' day with its emphasis on law, class and status. In the parable regarding the Good Samaritan, Jesus discloses that relationship to God is represented by behaviors which outweigh any particular religious doctrine that exhibit opposition to the purpose of God to restore His community of faithful; and to this end believers must demonstrate interest in the people God has created despite human religiosity (Luke 10: 25-37). The bureaucracy, evident in denominationalism, applies pressure on the para-church through disassociation and disfranchisement. Jesus' repudiation of divisive perspectives amongst God's people attests to the biblical support of cooperation between the church and the para-church.

The Divided Church

The official acknowledgement of theological and spiritual authority is the Holy Bible; some denominations include additional writings, while others may infer that the church leadership's analysis of Scripture is the final authority. Each in its own way has influenced biblical hermeneutics, redefining understanding and the works of the local church. A separation occurred between Christians globally. Christian communities in Eastern Europe and western Asia became known as Eastern Orthodox Churches and the Reformation Period divided western Christianity into Roman Catholic Church and Protestantism. During the Reformation Period contrasting emphases, interpretations, cultural, social and political influences promoted the development of factions culminating into differences expressed as denominations. The definition of denomination intimates an inharmonious perspective of Christian theology and within the universal body of Christ. In the nineteenth century certain religious denominations responded to the proliferation of denominational innovations, the development of non-denominational evangelical institutions and the growth of voluntary societies with antagonism. In essence, each organization was instituted with specific tenets as defined by the beliefs and practices of its own constituency; and although every protestant denomination maintains, to varying degrees, some form of relativity and visible unity with its member churches, there is radical decentralization. Denominational identity and statements of faith were incorporated to exclude Christians with different doctrinal convictions. The consequence has been "to create unified, self-governing and self-expressing communities" that have become a collection of subtly "warring tribes."[24] The multiplication of Christian institutions often results in factions, jealousy and rivalry. The effects of these transformations may have elicited the dilution of essential components of the church. There are now multitudinous Christian churches with separate ideologies instead of one universal Church having numerous locations which is supported by the Bible.

The doctrine of spiritual authority ensued following the advent of multiple, separate and distinct ideologies. The construct of conflict which has developed over spiritual authority precipitates hostilities. The inability to cooperate hinders the fulfillment of the Great Commission. Referring to John R. Mott's classic, *The Evangelism of the World in This Generation,* scholars contend that "the whole world could easily be evangelized if it were not for the wicked selfishness of Christians."[25] Frend asserts that "we still lack current views of Christianity" as we seek to interpret and comprehend the "Pauline Epistles and the traditions that lie behind the Gospels and Acts."[26] Following the Protestant Reformation to the current epoch of contemporary Christianity, church leadership consigns the local church as the spiritual authority and principle medium of ministry and mission. In the Book of Acts, three to five thousand individuals were converted to Christianity upon the arrival of the Holy Spirit. It is impractical to expect that the manifestation of gifts were solely expressed within the confines of a local house church, where the number of converts, which as Scripture states, "multiplied" regularly; or that these gifts could be utilized for God's service efficiently and effectively within this context alone; or that church leaders and those assigned by the church were the only ones to evangelize outsiders. The magnitude of the spiritually-gifted, sanctified masses would suggest the need for organized evangelical and missionary efforts as the message to "go into all the nations" attests. The Bible states, referencing spiritual gifts, that every believer receives the manifestation of the Spirit, distributed according to God's will (I Cor. 12:7, 11). But, throughout history mankind has demonstrated the tendency toward elitism. The humanity of Christians must be set aside to perform the tasks of the Spirit. The Bible contends that the sole authority of ministry and mission rests on the supernatural power of God who by His Spirit rules creation. The assertion is the created must not question the Creator but proceed according to the purpose of His will distinguished as children "of the living God" (Rom. 9: 14-26).

"Every kingdom divided against itself is brought to desolation; and every city or a house divided against itself cannot stand" (Mat. 12: 25). Biblical support for cooperation between the church and the para-church is its narrative that it is perilous to call that which is good, evil and that which is evil; good (Is. 5:20). It is even more dangerous to deny the presence of the Holy Spirit of God and to profess that the power of His Spirit is that of the enemy (Mat. 12: 31-32). Dissension and division insinuates there cannot be a church and a para- church. The church cannot endure the suggestion of half slave and half free represented by the doctrine of Spiritual authority which lacks biblical evidence. All believers are servants of the Most High. It is not expected that the Church will fall; the "gates of hell will not prevail against it" or that the local church will cease to exist, but the division is unbiblical and must end (Mark 16:18).

Unity of the Body Denied

The incongruity represented by the dissonance demonstrated between the church and the para-church is tantamount to the divisions, factions and separate sects such as the Sadducees, Pharisees and Essenes presented in Scripture. The para-church is viewed by the local church as an assembly having an "anti-ecclesiolatry and identification with the extreme individualism of the culture *which* appears to undermine the corporate power and authority of the local church."[27] Many Christian leaders refuse to recognize any authority above its local church, rejecting a visible unity of the universal Church though not denying the unity of an invisible universal Church as if they are separate and distinct. Therefore, contradicting the fact that the Bible attests to One God and "unity of the Spirit in the bond of peace" (Eph.4:1-6). The "claim of theological priority for the church, in both local and denominational expressions, and the doctrine of the priesthood of all believers" appears a paradox.[28] A puzzling self-contradiction or an impossible conundrum: the church cannot exist without the people of God, the people of God are the church, all of the people of God are the priesthood, yet the people of God are subordinate to the church. The opposition of local churches and larger church associations to the para-church may be due to the limited perspective from which para-church organizations are viewed. Recognized by some as vital to accomplishing specialized missions on behalf of the local church, the major concerns are authority, management and accountability. According to Charry, for the church, "the contemporaneity of the para-church may be off-putting because it undermines denominational and theological heritages."[29] Unquestionably, the para-church, which often offers introduction to spiritual points of view, is not the local church which is biblically designated as a place of community for foundational methodology, spiritual development and maturity (Eph. 4:12-16). The para-church usually establishes a central purpose with a clear direction to assure efficiency of operation in accomplishing specific ministry tasks. Often comprising a group of individuals from diverse churches, denominations, cultural and ethnic backgrounds it is held together by "one Lord, one faith and one baptism" (Eph. 4:5). The para-church transports ecumenism ahead of denominationalism in planning for the expression of Christian faith. Decidedly the laborer of the church, the para-church offers a window of opportunity for evangelizing. Moreover, in this forum, the model para-church necessitates an introduction to a local church. It has the capability, while engaging in evangelistic pursuits, to uphold biblical standards, reconstruct original beliefs; and institute efficacious practices and innovations, while the local church by its very nature is a buttress with the responsibility to maintain its integrity and the purity of the Gospel.

The profusion of new non-denominational churches and para-church groups evoke hostile reactions among many protestant religious groups. Focus on denominationalism appears to exacerbate divisiveness applying pressure on the unity of the faithful. Add the onslaught of advancing technologies, proliferating indifference and isolationism; and the traditional Christian orthodoxy of unity and wholeness becomes passé and hedonistic. The dynamic of contemporary American culture presents an increasingly competitive ecclesiastical and solitary society contradicting the collaboration, sharing and good stewardship of human, capital and financial resources obliged by Scripture of the Christian community (Acts 4:32,34-37; Rom. 15:25-26; I Cor. 16:1-2). Rick Warren contends that there are five tasks which Christ ordained for His church to accomplish as confirmed in Matthew 22: 37-40 and Matthew 28: 19-20.[30] These tasks may be identified as love God, love neighbor, make disciples, baptize them and instruct them in the Word of God. He emphasizes these principles through various Scriptures that give credence to para-church ministry exemplifying church membership demonstrating love through service in the community. The para-church being representative of the church as perhaps associates with the local church within a specific community will perform its duty because of mutual respect and acknowledgement of one unified purpose (Prov.19:21). According to the Book of Acts 2:1-47, the purposes of the New Testament Church include: worship, fellowship, edification, evangelism, and ministry. The para-church cannot provide the preordained culture of the Christian church; God, in Christ, has secured the identity, purpose and destiny of the local church. The particulars of each congregation include "matters of decision on the basis of what will help the church worship God best, what will help to establish an authentic Christian community and what will be the methods Christendom will demonstrate for a needy world."[31] Relinquished from preoccupation with works of salvation and the limitations imposed by Scriptural interpretation on the actions which determine an assembly of God, affords that individual members of the church can concentrate on the freedoms of service and evangelism by means of the para-church to discover successful methods of contact with individuals or groups outside of the church and maintain unity with the church.

The conflict relative to social, political, traditional, financial and territorial concerns does not subtract from the biblical accounts of the supernatural nature of the church. Each church is distinguished as "an organized institution; a true body politic with members fulfilling different functions" inclusive of "missionary expansion" and receiving assignment of specialized positions "for its orderly administration" all of "which traces its order to the will of God" (I Cor. 19:33).[32] It is a natural assumption that constructs formed in dissimilar social-historical context would be different. As noted, the mission of the church has sustained significant change. In terms of modernity, the church is conceived on the model of a society subject to hierarchical authority; while the model that prevailed prior to the reformation was a communion model. According to W.H.C. Frend, in the expanse of time "religion became a series of cult acts performed by professionals and priests."[33] Although societal changes and denominational divisiveness transformed the Church, its purposes have not changed and the role of the local church remains the same; an assembly of the elect having the reliable position of instructing, exhorting, rebuking, correcting and preparing believers for works of service, evangelism and discipleship.

According to historical and literary accounts, the para-church was created to fill a vacuum or to address a specific niche. Identified as a form of outsourcing some local churches and church associations rely on the para-church for Christian education materials, youth ministry resources and leadership training. Contemporary congregations raise and send money to Christian organizations to minister on behalf of those sending the money or chose to invest in neighborhood ministry through the use of discretionary funds for ministerial programs directed to the current generational paradigm of religiosity. Still, indicative of an irreverent integration of progressive-thinking principles there is mistrust and misconception within the local church leading para-church organizations to be limited, shackled and sometimes doomed to failure encumbered by the lack of support from the Body of Christ and fear of alienating the constituency to whom they look for resource support. Many church leaders have interwoven a consumerist orientation in the minds of its congregation contending the para-church misleads, compromises the gospel and is unbiblical due to the absence of specific church affiliation and accountability, causing a loss of community within the body of Christ. The para-church is developed to be a missionary movement exemplifying biblical teachings and standards through ethical and moral administration of its institutions in the delivery of products and services. Proclamation of the Gospel is readily available upon request and is presented as participant choice. The church has worship, proclamation, edification, exhortation and rebuke as its overarching mission. Each has responsibility in the plan of God and both exist to assist one another's development. Although para-church and local church partnerships may be identified as beneficial to evangelism, personal and spiritual growth and discipleship, often expressions of fear are displayed when consideration is given to para-church organizations superseding the local church in the priority and commitment of membership. To avert the fostering of social, political and organizational division, neither should be guided by an independent spirit of narcissism, humanism, or the desire for self-direction without accountability but by the expressed intent of the Word of God which advocates relationship with God and avows love amongst believers in the performance of God's divine purpose for His glory.

Chapter Summary

The Book of Ephesians instructs on the unity of believers in Jesus by referring to the integrality of the household of God. This book speaks of the communal colony comprised of Jews and Gentiles; the underlying message is indigenous of the entire Christian community. The Gentiles who were aliens and strangers have been united with the elect Jewish brothers and sisters through the blood of Christ. This also pervades the existence of contemporary Christians, for human intercession has been abolished by means of Christ's intervention and individual believers receive a Spiritual inheritance of sonship and priestly status enabling direct communication with the Father. Historically, a dividing wall existed to prevent the Gentiles from gaining entrance into the Jewish temple, and to enter beyond a particular point resulted in their death, Paul asserts that division has been shattered in Christ.

For Christ is our peace, who has made both one, and has broken down the middle wall of separation, having abolished in His flesh the enmity that is the law of commandments contained in ordinances so as to create in Himself one new man from the two, thus making peace and that He might reconcile them both to God in one body through the cross, thereby putting to death the enmity. For through Him we have access to one Spirit to the Father. (Eph. 2:14-18)

Believers are given access and authority through Jesus Christ. The limited perspective of some leaders is that an individual's vision must be managed through the church; otherwise its legitimacy is questioned. Sometimes the purpose and primary target for the endeavor is outside the geographical jurisdiction of the local church or contrary to the agenda of the leadership, yet requires cooperation from believers' community of faithful to attain and effectively perform. The limitations encountered by church leadership impose significant obstacles, deference of time and inhibition of exhaustive effort to engage potentially beneficial missionary work in God's schema. Since there is determined theological basis for unity in the body of Christ, Christian leadership of the church and the para-church should identify and acknowledge any undercurrents of dissatisfaction which forms the impetus of instituting para-church organizations. The church is criticized for being excessively oriented to programming and reputation; functioning as a social-political institution rather than an organized body of believers. There is concern that the local church is characterized by a generalized ministry, neglecting the specific needs of its Christian body. The Scriptural proposal for unification of the body and identifying every member as an integral functioning element is in opposition to the belief that the local church is God's single ally in His mission. The antagonism between believers, within the body of Christ and to outsiders, is reprehensible to God precipitating the need for cooperation.

The first Christian ministers were the apostles in the New Testament, to whom the living Lord revealed himself and sent "to the ends of the earth" *to be fruitful and multiply*; leading to the assignment of elders, deacons and pastors to provide oversight, spiritual accountability, service and teaching (Acts 1:8) The pastorate of every generation preach, commemorate, witness, and gather disciples in continuity with those early apostles. A central task of such representative ministry is personally and publicly to direct the local church, the people of God, to exhort and indoctrinate its dependence on Jesus Christ who is the source of its faith, mission, and unity. While authoritative offices and positions exist each is inherently a shared responsibility (Acts 15:22). According to Scripture, no minister is independent or autonomous (Rom. 12:5; Heb. 3: 3-4:2). Differences and intrusions of the Christian community by factions, multiculturalism and polity ultimately introduced a ministerial elite. Classification and investiture led to eventual triumph and has deposed laypersons of any authority or privileges in relation to many local congregations.[34] Denominationalism, for example, consigns different components of the various conceptual, philosophical and ideological exegesis identified in each local community inclusive of their representative "elders, pastors, bishops, priests and deacons," and regardless of presumptions expressing demarcation between laity and clergy, "these individuals are not of themselves the church."[35] Despite the dissension denominationalism educes, "religion permeates the life" of the believer in the Christian community and the church can conceivably be defined by a "theory of relationship" and "the totality of those who believe in and call on the name of Christ.[36] The declaration of the Word of God is that the multitude of faithful, as the disciples of Christ, are all to be an acknowledged priesthood and every local church, in spite of cultural and political philosophies is "judged to be constituted to this end under ONE authority" (Mat. 23: 8-10).[37] Requisite to spiritual growth and development of the Christian is the interrelatedness of the saints through the Spirit; all seek to teach and work together, and to express fellowship in support and care for each other.[38] This must be expressed by leadership across denominations, judicatories and associations to fulfill the ultimate plan of God for mankind. All believers, being saints of Christ have His directive; that in all nations disciples are to be replicated inclusive of baptizing them into the community of faith, Scriptural instruction and revelation in preparation for a future kingdom with God.

Is Christ divided? According to Scripture "there is no distinction, for the same Lord is Lord of all" (Rom. 10:12). This collegiality relates clergy and laity in a common mission. The contention throughout the Word of God is that the only authority is God and He ascertains, appoints and assigns of His own volition. Scripture attests to the totality and universality of God. God has set the agenda; therefore every believer is divinely enabled for specific purpose. Each institution is divinely assigned specific purpose. Neither is anyone of His without the empowerment of the Holy Spirit. Neither is exalted above the other. The functioning or malfunctioning of one part of the Body of Christ implicates another part as demonstrated in Scripture therefore; the biblical perspective supports cooperation between the church and the para-church.

CHAPTER 7

CONCLUSION

The para-church has always existed in some form without the label afforded it by contemporary society, the stigma as nonessential, "outside help," and truant to the church. Scripture attests the Church is an institution known as the body of Christ comprising individual members who adhere to the Word of God by the Holy Spirit with the principle that every Christian is a steward of divine trust having the acclaim as Spiritual heirs with Jesus. Historically, the church was enacted in places that would appear as unconventional by modern standards: outdoors, in marketplaces, by rivers, in schools and in private homes demonstrating that witnesses to the gospel message are not confined to *consecrated* buildings (Acts 8:29-35; 13:44; 16:13; 17:17; 19:9; 20:20). Accordingly, a believer's commission comes from the ultimate Source of authority and derives its legitimacy from Him. As a result of faith, every believer is enabled to perform the tasks which God has preordained for each of them (Eph. 2:10). Scripture attests that God, who has determined the years and environments of mankind, is to be the *one* preoccupation of every believer and His "Divine Nature" is not to be "shaped by man's devising" (Acts 17:26-29). Consequently, both commission and enablement are predicated upon the grace of God (John 3:27; Eph. 4:7-12). The Covenant of Grace is present for humankind and following acceptance the inheritance of the Holy Spirit is conveyed upon each believer for the execution of God's purposes. Biblical evidence which supports cooperation between the church and the para-church is demonstrated throughout the Bible and affirmed by Paul as the revelation of "the mystery hidden from ages and generations which is Christ" in every believer, "the hope of glory!"(Col.1: 25-27). For God did not give Jesus the Spirit by measure (John 3: 34). This significance is to be preached; admonishing and teaching everyone "with all wisdom," to empower believers everywhere to become mature with the same qualities and character of the teacher who is made perfect in Christ (Col. 1: 28). The commission to Spiritual maturity and discipleship is not optional in the advancement of God's Kingdom. Every believer is commissioned and enabled to advance this biblical standard as representatives of God in Christ, regardless of the visible institution from which ministry is accomplished.

The Church as the Visible Manifestation of God's Kingdom

The Church is assigned to be "an active presence of God in human history; caring, loving and supporting the lives of the individual and community life of the people with whom the Lord has made a covenant."[1] According to McGrath, Saint Augustine alleged that there are saints and sinners in the assembly, however "no one can come to Jesus unless drawn by the Father; and how can they come without hearing the Word of God" (John 6:44; Rom. 10:14).[2] "Every believer has a unique spiritual gift that God individually portions according to His sovereign will, design" and by His grace.[3] The Bible is persistent in its demand that all of the children of God utilize their spiritual giftedness in service for the Lord and it is the Lord who directs the engagement of service. Since sin and death is a fact of human existence, as disciples of Christ, the Church is to be concerned with the restoration and renewal of men and women to God. Christ offers righteousness through justification by grace through faith to overcome the penalty of sin, the receipt of the Holy Spirit and communion with God as the promised inheritance for every believer. The paradox of the church and the para-church is that the two are distinguishable components of the same reality. Just as the Father created man and woman with the instructions that although different we are one flesh and help to one another; this is also a model for the bride of Christ, the church (Gen. 2:18-24; Eph. 5:24-32). The same commission through different methodology is their divinely ordained task. Care must be exercised which prevents the church and the para-church from instituting "new doctrinal and linguistic orthodoxies in the name of pluralism and inclusivity."[4] In the Bible, the word *church* was designated to reference the body of Christian believers. The Holy Bible is the ultimate standard for critical evaluation of the purposes and function of the local church and the Church as a universal body. As constituents of the local church, the para-church exists to share with the local church the goal of the universal Church; to glorify God through Jesus Christ. Each group as an organized fellowship of Christians seeks to facilitate the mission of building God's Kingdom. However, this is where the similarity ends which is the reason for controversy between the church and the para-church. Understandably, each will differ in the particulars of strategy, philosophy and authority. The para-church as members of the body endeavors to be servants of Christ without excuse. It is written:

Let a man regard us in this manner, as servants of Christ, and stewards of the mysteries of God. It is required of stewards that one be found trustworthy. But it is a very small thing that I should be examined by you, or by any human court. The one who examines me is the Lord. Therefore do not go on passing judgment...learn not *to* exceed what is written, in order that no one of you might become arrogant in behalf of one against the other. For who regards you as superior? And what do you have that you did not receive? We are *judged as* fools for Christ's sake; but you are prudent in Christ; we are weak, but you are strong; you are distinguished, but we are without honor… and we toil…we endure…we try to conciliate. (I Cor. 4: 1-13; *emphasis mine*)

Jesus was born into a world of Jews, Gentiles, consumers and merchants who after His death would take the message of his life and teachings to the world. The dissemination of the message was presented within the synagogues, and houses; on hills, in valleys and ultimately in newly created church buildings. The Kingdom of God or the reign of God does not refer to a geographical location or to a specific political, social or economic system, it is representative of an alternative way, from previous social-religious nations, of comprehending who God is, what it means to be a God-created human and to belong to a community of the faithful.[5] It is the responsibility of the local church to provide "adequate grounding and accountability" for all of its constituents including enthusiastic, Spirit-guided potential leaders within the body of Christ enabling freedom in Christ to facilitate their assigned task.[6] Any distinction or characteristic of strength or awareness that has been entrusted to members of the body of Christ is to be used as complementary methods presenting as similitude of the astounding relationship that Christ has with His Church.

Beware of the Dogs

An overview of literature yields a wide range of perspectives regarding the para-church predicated upon strong philosophical and theological premises demonstrating consistent bias relative to perpetual misgivings regarding its identity. Scripture states: "Beware of the dogs...the evil workers; beware of the false circumcision" (Phil. 3:2). This is a contemptible phrase relative to malicious, deceitful laborers and false teachers who infiltrate the Church undermining the integrity of the Gospel; mingling the grace of God with the flesh and trusting in ordinances rather than the Spirit. Opponents to para-church, missions and volunteer societies state that there is no biblical relevance for them. They argue that "Scripture says nothing about missions as a means of evangelizing the world."[7] Organized efforts which are independent from specific church leadership are considered at odds with the church, rebelling against the authority of Christ and "investing themselves with the authority of the church even though they are not constituted as one."[8] The representative semantics of these arguments may be characterized as misunderstanding the dynamics of the Church in the Bible. There is no representation of an alternative church in the Bible, as some would acclaim. There is only ONE Church with many facets under ONE Authority. Even between institutions generally regarded as churches there are aberrations. Christ, as the verifiable commander-in-chief should be the mark of every church and the distinctiveness of faith, hope and love should never be sacrificed by the superficiality and self-absorption of humanity (I Cor. 13:13). An example of the biblical perspective which supports cooperation between the church and the para-church is the Holy Bible teaches that to effect evangelism and discipleship in the body of Christ and the world; Christianity must "not be polarized as differences in theology" and that "political-structural contexts are stumbling blocks to the restoration of God's Kingdom" (I Tim.1:4-7; Tit. 3:9).[9]

The antagonism of the local church presents as one superficially striving for salvation while promoting those things which cause division in the universal Church, the false teachings which create enmity by conjoining Christ with works, laws, and traditions of men. In Philippians 3:2, the false circumcision alludes to individuals who during the early Christian church sought to bind Christians under the laws of Judaism. Still, the life of the contemporary church continues to be wrought with insurgency which advances that righteousness can be obtained by mankind's efforts in keeping laws, customs, policy and ritual; that through division and supposition, exhorting man-made traditions and giving reign to the human nature which exalts position, status, class and authority, God shall be glorified. The church- para-church controversy is demonstrative of an adversarial relationship between the tradition of the Old Testament and the liberty of the New Testament. For example, Jesus affirmed: "the Sabbath was made for man, not man for the Sabbath" (Mark 2: 27). The revelation of God is given for the benefit of mankind; not for bondage (Rom. 8:15). Sabbath was to be provision in support of mankind's need to set aside time for God (Deut.5:13). However, the Jewish leaders instituted stipulations and requirements more rigid than God intended; condemning the innocent and having such zeal for righteousness, the religious leaders had become more stringent than the "Author and Finisher of faith" (Mark 2:23-24; 12:7; Heb. 12:2). Scripture declares: "The Son of Man is Lord even of the Sabbath" (Mark 2:28). Certainly, the laws, precepts and commandments have not been instituted to prohibit works for God's kingdom nor deeds of mercy. God has put His laws into the minds and hearts of all His children (Heb. 8:10). "Beware of the dogs…the false circumcision" denotes an emphasis on the carnal and not on serving God by the Spirit. All believers are responsible to adhere to the Holy Spirit.

A Shared Vision

The biblical perspective supports a shared vision and therefore, cooperation between the local church and the para-church. The Bible presents the church as an integrated system created by God and biblically substantiated as a complex structure (I Cor. 12). Much like other complex structures found in nature. Each member forming the church, is "fearfully and wonderfully made," and intricately aligned to be a suitable component in relationship (Ps.139:14; Rom. 12:4-5). Being transcendent, the church is not limited by the ideological, philosophical or theological views of humanity and as an interdependent system any isolated change within the organism will effect harm. Christian leaders, instructors and pastors have the responsibility to coordinate this system providing adequate grounding and accountability. The Word of God contends that every believer is called according to the will and purpose of God. Leadership has the responsibility for imparting exegetical and hermeneutical expression that highlights biblical truths and standards comprising the disciple's assignment, acceptance, initiation and implementation.

Assignment means a designated task or duty. It is an obligation. The Word of God states that the child of God is driven to accomplish the purpose of God. The Bible presents an empowering approach to Kingdom development and its sustainability. Christian leaders must ascertain the required task of believers. Therefore, leadership must be reminded that even an oracle is not speaking for God, but God is speaking through the oracle, taking care not to misuse the Words of the Lord (Jer.23:36, 39). In the Book of Jeremiah we observe the prophets who misdirected the Word of God, claiming he said things they wanted to be true. The Lord warned the people speaking "visions of their own heart that those who pervert His word will be forsaken and cast from his presence" (Jer. 14: 14-16; 23:16, 39-40). Leadership must use the Word of God for His purpose, not having a personal agenda; careful not to teach individual ideas apart from the Holy Bible. The premise of the Bible is that all God created are His and He is the authority distributing assignments. The Bible contends that the development of the kingdom of God renounces tradition, ritual, culture, ethnicity, denomination or class. Accordingly, the leadership position means empowerment, not control. Jesus exemplifies ultimate leadership of the church and the example for Christian leaders. He instructed everyone who listened and engaged many disciples empowering them for service in God's kingdom. Christ's example of empowerment leads to permission, transference, entrusting and commission which should be revealed throughout the body of Christ.

The Word of God states: "that love may abound in real knowledge and all discernment to approve the things that are excellent, in order to be sincere and blameless… to the glory and praise of God" (Phil. 1: 9-11). Christian leaders are to develop discernment to identify the call of God on someone's life for the furtherance of the gospel. Acknowledgement of being designated for specific task is the meaning of acceptance. Being the one God has called to manage those whom He has guided to a particular locale is a privilege and knowing that regardless of human motives "in every way, whether in pretense or in truth, Christ is proclaimed," every individual believer must be managed appropriately; as belonging to God (Phil. 11:18). Is Christ divided? Leadership is set apart to assist fellow heirs and spiritual priests in the acceptance of their assignment furnishing them with whatever is necessary for the undertaking (Eph. 4:11-16). They are to assist intellectually, socially, spiritually and sometimes financially in preparation for the journey (Rom. 12:13; I Cor. 8:1-9:15). The Bible proposes that the Christian leader should be conscious of his relationship with his disciples which must go beyond that of a teacher to become aware of the spiritual needs in his community (Mat. 7:21; 21:3; John 13:14; 15:20). Guided by the Holy Spirit which necessitates a common bond circumventing man-made perspectives of authority, the consciousness of Christian leadership is to be uniquely fashioned toward consummation of the Holy Kingdom (Matt. 16:27; 24:27, 30-31,36-44; Luke 18:8). According to Scripture, once the decision is made for God through Jesus Christ, every believer has an assignment, even the para-church, and local church leadership have the distinctive assignment of encouraging others to accept their specific assignment. Christian leaders should be willing to challenge their own thinking, mutually examine the thinking of others within the framework of love enabling parishioners to be open regarding their walk and accepting of their assignment.

The Christian leader, instructor and pastor assist the motivation of disciples during the initiation phase of the assignment. Initiation means acknowledging that the child of God is now suitable or fitted for the particular purpose. Initiation follows maturity. Utilizing the example of the Judean churches one must evaluate all who evangelize on the basis of their faithfulness to the true gospel (Gal.1). Once spiritually indoctrinated the individual begins the next road of the journey. (I Pet. 2:2; Rom.6). According to Scriptures, each member is a part of one another and is meant to support one another; to "be devoted in brotherly love, given preference in honor; contribute to the needs of one another and practice hospitality all in service of the Lord" (Rom. 12: 10-13). The church should not take on the territorialism and separation perspective of worldly institutions which projects a people whose primary concern is self-interests and individual survival. The Word of God presents a community perspective, although each local church is distinctive and separate, there is a common bond. Christian leadership has the invaluable responsibility to contribute toward building and developing the relevant Kingdom advocated in Scriptures. The Bible declares a shared vision with every believer given the commission of disseminating the gospel message, loving God and one another. Leadership must genuinely foster this shared vision by committing to the basic set of values proposed in Scripture. These values include honesty, openness, compassion and understanding. Christian leadership may need to assist in an organizing capacity during the initiation of the task. The Word of God promotes being other-centered instead of self-centered within the complexity of the body of Christ, a system steeped in history and tradition initiated by agape love (John 3:16).

Finally, the individual is enabled through the training and support of leadership to fulfill the assignment. Implementation is identified as materialization and sustained effort in action. The Bible promotes enthusiastic, Spirit-guided leadership which enables its disciple's freedom in Christ to facilitate their assigned task. Each constituent should be given freedom to create, to try one's own ideas and to be responsible for results. In this regard the leader offers prayer for the constituent as an equal, prayer for leadership to identify what support is needed and prayer to know how to assist with the spiritual growth, maturity and implementation of the assignment; which is not always directly from the church's *storehouse*. Each member having been endowed with spiritual gifts are commanded to utilize them for the benefit of the Kingdom. Christian leaders, instructors and pastors are noted in the Bible as having significant accountability to disciples. It does not promote the authoritarianism prevalent in contemporary society. This perspective promotes the expectation that the leader is the ultimate decision maker who has all of the answers. For some believers, this absolves them from responsibility leading to inhibited spiritual inaction for the gospel and individuals who simply sit on the pews with no ambition. God variously dispenses his gifts, and the differences between believers that they may honor Christ. All are His children and are accepted by Him. In John 21:15-17, Jesus commissions Peter in the role of leadership with the assignment to feed His lambs and tend to His sheep as a demonstration of Peter's love for Him. The agape love which Jesus conjures "has nothing to do with emotions. It has everything to do with intentions; a commitment to serve one another and a willingness to be vulnerable in the process."[10] As Oswald Chambers writes "our Lord comes steadily to us in every individual case asking the questions: Do you believe that I am able to do this? Do you really know the risen Lord? Do you know the power of the indwelling Spirit?[11] The Word of God challenges the faith of every Christian leader.

The divisive paradigm between the local church and the para-church is similar to the debate on creation. The existence of the universe and life is a fact; however, man has separated the methods of the origin of creation and life into two concepts. Debate ensues over the appropriate teaching in public schools. Evolution is presented as fact for the explanation of the origin of the universe and mankind, while overall, creation as depicted in the Bible is not presented in public schools. Here is an example of two seemingly relevant aspects to one major reality which causes dissension and masks the truth due to the volatility of division. As Christian leaders we must "cast down imaginations and every high thing that exalts itself against the knowledge of God, bringing into captivity every thought to the obedience of Christ (II Cor. 10). We must use our knowledge of God to destroy warped philosophies, demolish barriers to God's truths and construct our own minds, wills and emotions into the structure of life shaped by God in His Word and through the example of Jesus Christ. The Bible states that "God is love" (I John 4:8). The biblical perspective supports cooperation between the local church and the para-church. Is Christ divided? As leaders our own maturity is at stake, for the charge which is to be embraced is unity and love.

A New Attitude

The overarching premise of the Bible is that every believer must familiarize themselves with the God of relationship. Throughout its pages there are depictions of love, marriage, family, feasting and communion. We are reminded of God's sacrifice and love through Jesus who presented the Last Supper as communion for believers to commemorate an ongoing relationship with Him and each other. The animosity demonstrated by the church toward the para-church is contrary to the Word of God which demands that mankind love each other as they love themselves and to "contend earnestly for the faith" (Luke 10:27; Jude 1:3). The disunity displayed amongst believers requires a new attitude, "for it is the Sovereign Lord" who bestows His Spirit enabling His chosen people to be called "priests of the Lord and ministers of our God" (Is.61:6). His covenant is for the Church, not the idealized local church or the unconventional para-church. The two are the identified virgins awaiting the bridegroom, who must be equipped, organized and complete to enter the Kingdom of Heaven (Mat. 25:1-13).

In an effort to effect change in attitude there is a need for new terminology to define and label the para-church. This term confuses church congregations and places Christian ministry outside of the church which inhibits collaboration between believers to advance the cause of Christ. Division in the body of Christ, in any form is profoundly problematic. There is a need for dialogue to overcome the dissension, to decidedly remove the prefix para and to acknowledge that we are all the church. Christ is the context and the content of the Christian faith and the rationale for the biblical perspective which supports cooperation between the church and the para-*church*. The para-church is the missions, community outreach society or ministry arm of the church. It is not the institution called church but is the people called church on Divine assignment to do the work that is expressed through the Holy Spirit by the institution called church. The opposition from the church constructs the anomaly of their relationship. Divergent Scriptural interpretation cannot displace the fact that there is only One Body which is the composite of every believer not referencing vocation, baptism, or Christian affiliation. The Bible emphatically opposes disunity in the Church furthering the pronouncement of a biblical perspective supporting cooperation between the church and the para-church; as both constitute the Church. The body of Christ with all of its diverse components is the visible Christ instituted in the plan of God to develop His Kingdom. The dissonance wrought by denominationalism, orthodoxy, jurisdiction and the para-church classification begs the question: Is Christ divided?

ABOUT THE AUTHOR

Dr. Felecia Rodgers is the founder and president of a grassroots, nonprofit charitable organizations which conducts community outreach ministry throughout Greater Cleveland. She has earned a doctorate of Philosophy (Ph.D.) at the Trinity Theological Seminary in Indiana, Masters in Public Administration (MPA) and B.A. at Cleveland State University. Dr. Rodgers is the author of *Grafted Inn*, a drama addressing the different perspectives people have regarding the message of the Bible. She coordinates seminars, conferences and workshops; and teaches on biblical theology, spiritual growth and discipleship. Dr. Rodgers resides with her husband in Cleveland Ohio.

ACKNOWLEDGEMENTS

All glory to God for the many things that He has done in and through my life!

It is my hope that these pages are a critical resource for church leaders, Christian educators, ministry leaders, para church organizations and others interested in bibliographical research surrounding the local church- para church anomaly. I trust that there has been enlightenment as you searched the text and the Word of God to confirm biblical support for cooperation between the local church and the para-church expressed as unity, relationship through One Lord, One Spirit, One baptism, individual commission and accountability in the purposes of God for His kingdom.

Special thanks to Dr. Marc Royer, pastor, teacher, author and the president of The Christian Resource Group, for his exhortation to press forward with this project to wherever God is leading and for the sincere and orthodox theological perspective of Dr. Max Sturdivant, Jr., Dean of Faculty Development Trinity College of the Bible and Theological Seminary.

I also would like to acknowledge Mr. Melvin Frazier, a friend who would often obtain the texts and other publications for me when limited by circumstances, Evangelist Janice Renee Erving and all of my brothers and sisters in Christ for their support and prayers. I am indebted to all of my colleagues who support and struggle to sustain outreach ministry defined as the para-church. Remain steadfast unto God striving for the high calling in Christ Jesus our Lord.

Finally, words cannot express the appreciation owed my husband Robert, for his love of God demonstrated by his devotion, confidence and encouragement; without whom I could not undertake my ministry.

Praise be to the God and Father of our Lord Jesus Christ! In his great mercy he has given us new birth into a living hope through the resurrection of Jesus Christ from the dead (I Pet. 1:3).

NOTES

INTRODUCTION

1. James C. G. Greig. "The New Testament and Christian Origins," <u>Interpreter's One-Volume Bible Commentary</u>, Edited by Charles M. Laymon, Nashville: Abingdon Press, 1980. 1190

2. Ibid.

3. Richard Taylor. <u>How to Read a Church</u>, Mahwah NJ: Hidden Springs, 2003. 9

4. Daniel G. Reid. <u>Concise Dictionary of Christianity in America</u>, Eugene OR: Wipf and Stock Publishers, 1995. 210

5. Frederick Norwood. "The Early History of the Church," in <u>The Interpreter's One Volume Commentary of the Bible</u>, Ed. Charles Layman, Nashville, TN: Abingdon Press, 1980. 1045

6. David Stanley, S.J. "The Greco-Roman Background of the New Testament," in <u>The Interpreter's One Volume Commentary on the Bible</u>, Ed. Charles Layman, Nashville, TN: Abingdon Press, 1980. 1037

7. Thomas M. Messner. "Can Para church Organizations Hire and Fire on the Basis of Religion Without Violating Title VII?" <u>University of Florida Journal of Law and Public Policy</u> 17, No. 1 (April 2006): 69

8. Wesley K. Wilmer, David J. Schmidt, Martin Smith. <u>The Prospering Parachurch</u>, San Francisco: Jossey Bass Publisher, 1998. Xii

9. Ibid.

10. Ibid., 43

11. Ibid., 27

12. John S. Hammett. "How Church and Parachurch Should Relate: Arguments for a Servant-Partnership Model." <u>Missiology: An International Review,</u> Vol. XXVIII, No. 2 (April 2000): 200

13. Ellen T. Charry. "Will There Be a Protestant Center?" <u>Theology Today</u> 57 No. 4 (Jan. 2001): 453-58

14. John G. Stackhouse. <u>Evangelical Landscapes: Facing Critical Issues of the Day</u>, Grand Rapids: Baker Academic, 2002. 45

15. Ibid.

16. Ibid., 68

17. G. J. Wenham, et al., New Bible Commentary, Downers Grove, Ill.: Intervarsity Press, 1994. 1

18. William Yarchin. <u>History of Biblical Interpretation,</u> Peabody, Mass: Hendrickson Publishers, 2004. Vi

19. G. J. Wenham, et al., 1

CHAPTER ONE

The Church as a Communal Colony

1. Jonathan R. Wilson. <u>Why Church Matters: Worship, Ministry and Mission in Practice</u>, Grand Rapids: Brazos Press, 2006. 13

2. Ibid., 88

3. Ibid., 93

4. Elmer L. Townes. <u>Bible Answers for Almost All Your Questions</u>, Nashville: Thomas Nelson Publishers, 2003. 103

5. Sherman E. Johnson. "The New Testament and The Christian Community," In <u>The Interpreter's One Volume Commentary of the Bible</u>, Edited by Charles Layman, Nashville, TN: Abingdon Press, 1980. 1116

6. William H. Brackney. <u>Christian Voluntarism: Theology and Praxis</u>, Grand Rapids: Wm. B.Eerdmans Publishing Company, 1997. 123

7. Jacob Neusner, Bruce Chilton, William Graham. <u>Three Faiths, One God</u>, Boston: Brill Academic Publishers, Inc. 2002. 148

8. Ibid., 149

9. James Strong. The New Strong's Concordance, Nashville: Thomas Nelson Publishers, 1990. 20

10. Ibid., 71

11. G.J. Wenham, J.A. Motyer, D. A. Carson, R.T. France. <u>New Bible Commentary</u>, Downers Grove, Ill.: Inter-Varsity Press, 1994. 437

12. Vine, W.E. <u>Vine's Complete Expository Dictionary</u>, Nashville: Thomas Nelson Publishers, 1996. 614

13. R. Newton Flew. <u>Jesus and His Church</u>, London: The Epworth Press, 1960. 16

14. Strong, 200, 52

15. Flew, 36

16. Ibid., 38

17. Ibid., 40

18. Wenham, et al., 1078

19. Ibid., 1066

20. Lawrence B. Porter. <u>A Guide to the Church</u>, Staten Island, NY: the Society of St. Paul/Alba House, 2008. 82

21. Samuel Terrien. "The Religion of Israel," In <u>The Interpreter's One Volume Commentary of the Bible</u>, Edited by Charles Layman, Nashville, TN: Abingdon Press, 1980. 1158

22. Vine, 71

23. Jonathan R. Wilson, <u>Why Church Matters: Worship, Ministry and Mission in Practice</u>, Grand Rapids: Brazos Press, 2006. 92

24. Ibid.

25. Ibid., 11

26. Frederick Abbott Norwood. "The Early History of the Church," In <u>The Interpreter's One Volume Commentary of the Bible</u>, Edited by Charles Layman, Nashville, TN: Abingdon Press, 1980. 1046

27. Terrien, 1157

28. Neusner, etal., 5

29. Ibid., 115-116

30. Ibid., 127

31. Ibid., 116

32. Vine, 42-43, 122

33. Charles M. Laymon. "The New Testament Interpretation of Jesus," In The Interpreter's One Volume Commentary of the Bible, Edited by Charles Layman, Nashville, TN: Abingdon Press, 1980. 1174

34. The American Heritage Dictionary of the English Language Fourth Edition, Boston MA: Houghton Mifflin Company, 2005.

35. Douglas Harper. "Church". Online Etymology Dictonary, Retrieve on 2008-10-13

36. W. H. C. Frend. The Early Church, London: SCM Press, LTD, 1991. 38

37. Ibid., 43

38. Comby, Jean. How to Read Church History, Vol. One, New York: Crossroad Publishing Company, 1990. 19

39. Michael G. Lawler. What Is And What Ought To Be, New York: Continuum International Publishing Group, Inc. 2005. 91

40. Ibid.

41. Ibid., 97

42. Ibid., 100

43. Ibid., 11

44. Robert C. Dentan. "The Kingdom of God in the Old Testament," In The Interpreter's One Volume Commentary of the Bible, Edited by Charles Lyman, Nashville, TN: Abingdon Press, 1980. 1159

45. Comby, 36

CHAPTER TWO
The Spiritual Inheritance of Believers

1. W.E. Vine. Vine's Complete Expository Dictionary, Nashville: Thomas Nelson Publishers, 1996. 325

2. Ibid.

3. Oswald Chambers. <u>The Complete Works of Oswald Chambers</u>, Grand Rapids: Discovery House Publishers, 2000. 921

4. Samuel J. Mikolaski. "The Theology of the New Testament," In <u>The Expositor's Bible Commentary, Vol.1</u>, edited by Frank E. Gaebelein. Grand Rapids: Zondervan, 1979. 463

5. Ibid.

6. Massey H. Shepherd, Jr. "The Gospel According to John," In <u>The Interpreter's One Volume Commentary of the Bible</u>, Edited by Charles Layman, Nashville, TN: Abingdon Press, 1980. 724

7. Jacob Neusner, et al. <u>Three Faiths, One God</u>, Boston: Brill Academic Publishers, Inc. 2002. 178

8. Henry T. Blackaby and Claude V. King, <u>Experiencing God</u>, Nashville, TN: Broadman and Hollman Publishers, 1994. 86

9. Vine. 196

10. Ibid., 545

11. Mikolaski. 469

12. R. Newton Flew. <u>Jesus and His Church</u>. London: The Epworth Press, 1960. 156

13. Mikolaski. 468

14. Neusner. 224

15. Ibid., 140

16. Charles Spurgeon. <u>Being God's Friend</u>, New Kensington, PA: Whittaker House, 1997. 97

17. Spiros Zodhiates. <u>Hebrew-Greek Key Word Study Bible</u>: New American Standard, Chattanooga, TN: AMG Publishers, 1990. 1397

18. Mikolaski., 467

19. Ibid., 469, 471

20. Guy D. Nave, Jr. <u>The Role and Function of Repentance in Luke-Acts</u>, Atlanta: Society of Biblical Literature, 2002. 22

21. John MacArthur. <u>The MacArthur Study Bible: New American Standard Bible</u>, Nashville: Thomas Nelson Inc., 2006. 117

22. Chambers. 927, *emphasis mine*

23. Flew, 159

24. Charles F. Pfeiffer and Everett F. Harrison. <u>The Wycliffe Bible Commentary</u>, Chicago: Moody Press, 1990. 1127

25. Flew, 158

26. Pfeiffer and Harrison, 1127

27. G.J. Wenham, et al. <u>New Bible Commentary</u>, Downers Grove, Ill.:Inter-Varsity Press, 1994. 40

28. Vine, 54

29. Ibid., 487

30. Ibid., 486

31. Claude Holmes Thompson. "The First Letter of Peter," In <u>The Interpreter's One Volume Commentary of the Bible</u>, Edited by Charles Layman, Nashville, TN: Abingdon Press, 1980. 927

32. Jean Comby and Diarmaid MacCulloch. <u>How to Read Church History Vol. Two,</u> New York: Crossroad Publishing Company, 1989. 134

33. Ibid., 111

34. Ibid., 110

35. Ibid.

36. Flew, 155

37. Pfeiffer, 1048

38. Mikolaski, 466

39. Flew, 118

40. Blackman, Edwin Cyril. "The Letter of Paul to the Romans," In <u>The Interpreter's One Volume Commentary of the Bible</u>, Edited by Charles Layman, Nashville, TN: Abingdon Press, 1980. 783

41. Ibid., 769

42. Pfieffer, 1108

43. Blackmon, 410

44. Flew, 118

45. "position." Encyclopedia Britannica. 2009. Encyclopedia Britannica Online. 21 Jun. 2009 <http:// www.britanica.com/ EBchecked/topic/551450/social-status>

CHAPTER THREE
The Emergence of the Para Church

1. Alister E. McGrath. Christian Theology: An Introduction, Malden, MA: Blackwell Publishing, 2001. 62

2. Jonathan R. Wilson Why Church Matters: Worship, Ministry and Mission in Practice, Grand Rapids: Brazos Press, 2006. 144

3. Ibid., 153

4. Victor Paul Furnish. "The New Testament Interpretation of Jesus," In The Interpreter's One Volume Commentary of the Bible, Edited by Charles Layman, Nashville, TN: Abingdon Press, 1980. 843

5. John G. Stackhouse Jr. Evangelical Landscapes: Facing Critical Issues of the Day, Grand Rapids: Baker Academic, 2002. 27

6. Jerry White. The Church and the Para church: An Uneasy Marriage, Portland: Multnomah Press, 1983. 36

7. Ibid., 46, 47

8. Ibid., 48

9. Ibid.

10. Ibid, 37; Luther E. Copeland, "Who Really Sent the First Missionaries?" Evangelical Missions Quarterly 11:4, (1975) 233-239

11. Thomas M. Messner. "Can Para church Organizations Hire and Fire on the Basis of Religion without Violating Title VII?" University of Florida Journal of Law and Public Policy 17, No. 1 (April 2006): 67

12. Ibid.

13. White, 50

14. Ibid., 51

15. McGrath, 5-7

16. William Yarchin. <u>History of Biblical Interpretation,</u> Peabody, Mass: Hendrickson Publishers, 2004. Xi

17. www.barna.org/ barna-update/article/5-barna-update/182-christian-mass-media-reach-more-adults-with-the Christian-message-than-do-churches.html (5/1/2009).

18. www.barna.org/barna-update/article/5-barna-update/182-one-in-three-adults-is-unchurched.html (5/1/2009).

19. Ibid.

20. Ibid.

21. Mathis, James R. "The Making of the Primitive Baptists," In <u>Studies in American Popular History and Culture</u>, edited by Jerome Nadelhaft, New York: Routledge, 2004. 35

22. Ibid.

23. McGrath, 534

24. Ibid.

25. David E. Fitch. <u>The Great Giveaway</u>, Grand Rapids: Baker Books, 2005. 16

26. Mathis, 35

27. Fitch, 13-14

28. Charles Spurgeon. <u>Being God's Friend</u>, New Kensington, PA: Whittaker House, 1997. 58

29. Ibid., 59

30. Thomas M. Messner. "Can Para church Organizations Hire and Fire on the Basis of Religion without Violating Title VII?" <u>University of Florida Journal of Law and Public Policy</u> 17, No. 1 (April 2006): 7

31. David Kinnaman, and Gabe Lyons,. <u>Un Christian: What a New Generation Really Thinks About Christianity... And Why It Matters</u>, Grand Rapids: Baker Books, 2007. 206

32. Messner, 63-65

33. Darrell L. Guder et al. <u>Missional Church</u>, Grand Rapids:William B. Eerdmans Publishing Company,1998. 1

34. McGrath, 535

CHAPTER FOUR

The Controversy: Local Church Perspective on the Para Church

1. Homer Duncan. The Divine Intent, Lubbock, TX: The Worldwide Missionary Crusader, 1982. 3

2. Samuel J. Mikolaski. "The Theology of the New Testament," In The Expositor's Bible Commentary, Vol.1, edited by Frank E. Gaebelein. Grand Rapids: Zondervan, 1979. 478

3. Ibid.

4. Charles R.Taber, To Understand the World, To Save the World, Harrisburg, PA: Trinity Press International, 2000. 10

5. Ibid., 12

6. Duncan, 1

7. Mikaloski, 477

8. Ibid., 478

9. Jacob Neusner, Bruce Chilton, William Graham. Three Faiths, One God, Boston: Brill Academic Publishers, Inc. 2002. 235

10. McGonigle, Thomas D., Quigley, James F. A History of the Christian Tradition, New York: Paulist Press, 1988. 65

11. Neusner, et al, 234-235

12. Mikaloski, 479

13. Ibid., 478

14. Ellen, T. Charry. "Will There Be a Protestant Center?" Theology Today 57, no. 4 (Jan. 2001). 454

15. Ibid., 32

16. Darrell L. Guder, et al. Missional Church, Grand Rapids: William B. Eerdmans Publishing Company, 1998.66

17. Frances E. Kearns, "Teaching The Bible to Youth and Adults." In The Interpreter's One Volume Commentary of the Bible, Edited by Charles Layman, Nashville, TN: Abingdon Press, 1980. 1265

18. Guder, 6

19. Stackhouse, 32

20. Charles R. Taber, <u>To Understand the World, To Save the World</u>, Harrisburg, PA: Trinity Press International, 2000. 103

21. Alan Neely. "Religious Pluralism: Threat or Opportunity for Mission?" <u>Mission at the Dawn of the 21st Century: A Vision For the Church,</u> edited by Paul Varo Martinson, Minneapolis: Kirk House Publishers, 1999. 39

22. Taber, 135

23. David Kinnaman, and Gabe Lyons. <u>Un Christian: What a New Generation Really Thinks About Christianity… And Why It Matters</u>, Grand Rapids: Baker Books, 2007. 217

24. William H. Brackney, <u>Christian Voluntarism: Theology and Praxis</u>, Grand Rapids: Wm. B. Eerdmans Publishing Company, 1997. 110

25. Tabor, 207

26. Wesley K.Wilmer, J. David Schmidt, Martyn Smith. <u>The Prospering Para church</u>, San Francisco: Jossey-Bass Publishers, 1998. 13

27. White, 85

28. Charry, 454

29. James R. Mathis. "The Making of the Primitive Baptists," In <u>Studies in American Popular History and Culture</u>, edited by Jerome Nadelhaft, New York: Routledge, 2004.78

30. Wilmer, 11

31. Claude E. Payne and Hamilton Beazley. <u>Reclaiming the Great Commission</u>, San Francisco: Jossey-Bass, 2000. 49

32. Mathis, 79-81

33. Charry, 453-54

34. Lyle E. Schaller. <u>The New Context for Ministry</u>, Nashville: Abingdon Press, 2002. 179

35. Max Weber,. <u>The Protestant Ethic and the Spirit of Capitalism</u>, Chicago: Fitzroy Dearborn Publishers, 2001. 32

36. Ibid., 33

37. Charry, 456

38. G.J. Wenham, J.A. Motyer, D. A Carson, R.T. France. <u>New Bible Commentary</u>, Downers Grove, Ill.: InterVarsity Press, 1994. 1388

39. White 25

40. Jerry White. <u>The Church and the Para church: An Uneasy Marriage</u>, Portland: Multnomah Press, 1983. 85

41. Ibid., 82

42. John G. Stackhouse Jr. <u>Evangelical Landscapes: Facing Critical Issues of the Day</u>, Grand Rapids: Baker Academic, 2002. 43

43. Israel Selvanayagam. "Towards an Evangelical Theology for a Pluralist Age," <u>Mission at the Dawn of the21st Century: A Vision For the Church,</u> edited by Paul Varo Martinson, Minneapolis: Kirk House Publishers, 1999. 215

CHAPTER FIVE

The Integral Relationship Between the Local Church and the Para Church

1. Richard J. Foster. <u>Celebration of Discipline</u>. San Francisco: Harper & Row, Publishers, 1988. 115

2. Wilmer, 10

3. Ibid.

4. Rick Warren. <u>The Purpose Driven Church</u>, Grand Rapids: Zondervan, 1995. 365

5. Ibid., 367-8

6. Oswald Chambers. <u>The Complete Works of Oswald Chambers</u>, Grand Rapids: Discovery House Publishers, 2000. 247

7. Selvanayagam, 205

8. Payne, 10

9. Ibid., 12

10. Ibid.

11. Ibid., 18

12. Leander E. Keck, "The Letter of Paul to the Philippians." In The Interpreter's One Volume Commentary of the Bible, Edited by Charles Layman, Nashville, TN: Abingdon Press, 1980. 850

13. Payne, 11

14. David B. Barrett and Todd M. Johnson. World Christian Trends AD 30-2200, Pasadena, CA: WilliamCarey Library, 2001. 3

15. Charles Colson and Nancy Pearcey. How Now Shall We Live? Wheaton, IL: Tyndale House Publishers, Inc. 1999. 302

16. Barnett and Johnson, 6

17. Hammett, John S. "How Church and Para church Should Relate: Arguments for a Servant-Partnership Model," Missiology: An International Review, Vol. XXVIII, No. 2 (April 2000). 200

18. Barnett and Johnson, 5

19. Ibid.

20. Ibid.

21. Saint Augustine. The City of God, New York: The Modern Library, 2000. 344

22. Ibid., 346

23. Alister E. McGrath. Christian Theology: An Introduction, Malden, MA: Blackwell Publishing, 2001. 557

24. Barnett and Johnson, 860

25. Payne, 192

26. Ibid.

27. Foster, 112

CHAPTER SIX

Malfunctioning of one part implicates another part

1. Timothy C. Morgan. "Re-Neighboring Our Cities," Christianity Today vol. 40 (January 8, 1996). 15

2. Ibid.

3. Ibid.

4. Rick Warren. <u>The Purpose Driven Church</u>, Grand Rapids: Zondervan, 1995. 365

5. Ibid., 310

6. Leith Anderson. <u>Leadership that Works: Hope and Direction for Church and Para church Leaders in Today's Complex World</u>, Minneapolis: Bethany House Publishers, 1999. 48

7. Morgan, 16

8. Warren, 342

9. Morgan, 16

10. Warren, 331

11. Henry T. Blackaby and, Claude V. King. <u>Experiencing God</u>, Nashville, TN: Broadman and Hollman Publishers, 1994. 205

12. David E. Fitch. <u>The Great Giveaway</u>, Grand Rapids: Baker Books, 2005. 43

13. Ibid., 49-50

14. John G. Stackhouse Jr. <u>Evangelical Landscapes: Facing Critical Issues of the Day</u>, Grand Rapids: Baker Academic, 2002. 45

15. David B. Barrett and Todd M. Johnson. <u>World Christian Trends AD 30-2200</u>, Pasadena, CA: William Carey Library, 2001. 851

16. Stackhouse Jr., 32

17. Ibid

18. Warren, 79

19. Ibid., 80

20. Charles A. Tidwell. <u>Church Administration Effective Leadership for Ministry</u>, Nashville: Broadman Press, 1985. 27

21. Claude E. Payne and Hamilton Beazley. <u>Reclaiming the Great Commission</u>, San Francisco: JosseyBass, 2000. 21

22. Ibid., 22-23

23. Richard Taylor. <u>How to Read a Church</u>, Mahwah, NJ: Hidden Springs, 2003. 9

24. Lyle E. Schaller. <u>The New Context for Ministry</u>, Nashville: Abingdon Press, 2002. 45-47

25. David B. Barrett and Todd M. Johnson. <u>World Christian Trends AD 30-2200</u>, Pasadena, CA: William Carey Library, 2001. 663

26. W. H. C. Frend. <u>The Early Church</u>, London: SCM Press, LTD, 1991. 1

27. Ellen, T. Charry. "Will There Be a Protestant Center?" <u>Theology Today</u> 57, no. 4 (Jan. 2001): 455

28. John S. Hammett "How Church and Para church Should Relate: Arguments for a Servant-Partnership Model," <u>Missiology: An International Review</u>, Vol. XXVIII, No. 2 (April 2000): 199

29. Charry, 453-54

30. Rick Warren. <u>The Purpose Driven Church</u>, Grand Rapids: Zondervan, 1995. 102-106

31. John G. Stackhouse Jr. <u>Evangelical Landscapes: Facing Critical Issues of the Day</u>, Grand Rapids: Baker Academic, 2002. 22

32. R. Newton Flew. <u>Jesus and His Church</u>. London: The Epworth Press, 1960. 156

33. Frend, 9

34. Jean Comby and Diarmaid MacCulloch. <u>How to Read Church History Vol. Two,</u> New York: Crossroad Publishing Company, 1989.174

35. Ibid., 148

36. Ibid., 174

37. Ibid.

38. Blackaby and King, 210

CHAPTER SEVEN
Conclusion

1. Thomas D McGonigle. James F. Quigley. <u>A History of the Christian Tradition</u>, New York:Paulist Press, 1988. 52

2. Alister E. McGrath. <u>Christian Theology: An Introduction</u>, Malden, MA: Blackwell Publishing, 2001. 480

3. John MacArthur,. <u>The MacArthur Study Bible: New American Standard Bible</u>, Nashville: Thomas Nelson Inc., 2006. 1777

4. McGrath, 456

5. McGonigle 52

6. Jerry White. <u>The Church and the Para church: An Uneasy Marriage</u>, Portland: Multnomah Press, 1983. 25

7. James R. Mathis. "The Making of the Primitive Baptists," In <u>Studies in American Popular History and Culture</u>, edited by Jerome Nadelhaft, New York: Routledge, 2004. 77

8. Ibid., 79

9. Barrett and Johnson, 853

10. Peter M. Senge, <u>The Fifth Discipline</u>, New York: Doubleday Currency, 1990. 285

11. Chambers, 1309

BIBLIOGRAPHY

American Psychololgical Assoication (APA):shema. (n.d). Dictionary. com Unabridged (v.1.1). Retrieved March 27, 2009, from website: http:// dictionary.reference.com/browse/shema

Anderson, Leith. Leadership that Works: Hope and Direction for Church and Para church Leaders in Today's Complex World, Minneapolis: Bethany House Publishers, 1999.

Barrett, David B. and Johnson, Todd M. World Christian Trends AD 30-2200, Pasadena, CA: William Carey Library, 2001.

Blackaby, Henry T. and King, Claude V. Experiencing God, Nashville, TN: Broadman and Hollman Publishers, 1994.

Blackman, Edwin Cyril. "The Letter of Paul to the Romans," In The Interpreter's One Volume Commentary of the Bible, Edited by Charles Layman, Nashville, TN: Abingdon Press, 1980. 768-794

Brackney, William H. Christian Voluntarism: Theology and Praxis, Grand Rapids: Wm. B. Eerdmans Publishing Company, 1997.

Camp, Bruce K. "A Theological Examination of the Two-Structure Theory," Missiology: An International Review, Vol. XXIII, No. 2 (April 1995): 197-209

Chambers, Oswald. The Complete Works of Oswald Chambers, Grand Rapids: Discovery House Publishers, 2000.

Charry, Ellen, T., "Will There Be a Protestant Center?" <u>Theology Today</u> 57, no. 4 (Jan. 2001): 453-58.

Cole, Neil. <u>Organic Church: Growing Faith Where Life Happens</u>, San Francisco: Jossey-Bass, 2005.

Colson, Charles & Pearcey, Nancy. <u>How Now Shall We Live?</u> Wheaton, IL: Tyndale House Publishers, Inc. 1999.

Comby, Jean. <u>How to Read Church History,Vol. One,</u> New York: Crossroad Publishing Company, 1990.

Comby, Jean, MacCulloch, Diarmaid. <u>How to Read Church History Vol. Two,</u> New York: Crossroad Publishing Company, 1989.

Copeland, Luther E. "Who Really Sent the First Missionaries?" <u>Evangelical Missions Quarterly</u> 11:4, (1975) 233-239

Dentan, Robert C. "The Kingdom of God in the Old Testament," <u>Interpreter's One-Volume Bible Commentary</u>, Edited by Charles M. Laymon, Nashville: Abingdon Press, 1980. 1159-1166

Duncan, Homer. <u>The Divine Intent</u>, Lubbock, TX: The Worldwide Missionary Crusader, 1982.

Fitch, David E. <u>The Great Giveaway</u>, Grand Rapids: Baker Books, 2005.

Flew, R. Newton. <u>Jesus and His Church</u>. London: The Epworth Press, 1960.

Foster, Richard J. <u>Celebration of Discipline</u>. San Francisco: Harper & Row, Publishers, 1988.

Frend, W. H. C. <u>The Early Church</u>, London: SCM Press, LTD, 1991.

Furnish, Victor Paul. "The New Testament Interpretation of Jesus," In <u>The Interpreter's One Volume Commentary of the Bible</u>, Edited by Charles Layman, Nashville, TN: Abingdon Press, 1980. 834-844

Greig, James C. G. "The New Testament and Christian Origins," <u>Interpreter's One-Volume Bible Commentary</u>, Edited by Charles M. Laymon, Nashville: Abingdon Press, 1980. 1187-1193

Guder, Darrell L., et al. Missional Church, Grand Rapids: William B. Eerdmans Publishing Company, 1998.

Hamilton, Michael S. "We're in the Money!" Christianity Today 44, No. 7 (June 12, 2000): 36-43.

Hammett, John S. "How Church and Para church Should Relate: Arguments for a Servant-Partnership Model," Missiology: An International Review, Vol. XXVIII, No. 2 (April 2000): 199-207

Harper, douglas, "church". Online Etymology Dictonary, Retrieve on 2008-10-13. "Gk. *kyriakon* (adj.) "of the Lord" was used of houses of Christian worship since c.300, especially in the East, though it was less common in this sense than *ekklesia* or *basilike.*"

Johnson, Sherman E. "The New Testament and The Christian Community," In The Interpreter's One Volume Commentary of the Bible, Edited by Charles Layman, Nashville, TN: Abingdon Press, 1980. 1116-1123

Keck, Leander E. "The Letter Of Paul To The Philippians." In The Interpreter's One Volume Commentary of the Bible, Edited by Charles Layman, Nashville, TN: Abingdon Press, 1980. 845-855

Kearns, Frances E. "Teaching The Bible to Youth and Adults." In The Interpreter's One Volume Commentary of the Bible, Edited by Charles Layman, Nashville, TN: Abingdon Press, 1980. 1264-1268

Kinnaman, David and Lyons, Gabe. Un Christian: What a New Generation Really Thinks About Christianity... And Why It Matters, Grand Rapids: Baker Books, 2007.

Lawler, Michael G. What Is And What Ought To Be, New York: Continuum International Publishing Group, Inc. 2005.

Laymon, Charles M. "The New Testament Interpretation of Jesus," In The Interpreter's One Volume Commentary of the Bible, Edited by Charles Layman, Nashville, TN: Abingdon Press, 1980. 1167-1175

MacArthur, John. The MacArthur Study Bible: New American Standard Bible, Nashville: Thomas Nelson Inc., 2006.

Malherbe, Abraham J. Social Aspects of Early Christianity, Philadelphia: Fortress Press, 1983.

Mathis, James R. "The Making of the Primitive Baptists," In <u>Studies in American Popular History and Culture</u>, edited by Jerome Nadelhaft, New York: Routledge, 2004.

McGonigle, Thomas D., Quigley, James F. <u>A History of the Christian Tradition</u>, New York: Paulist Press, 1988.

McGrath, Alister E. <u>Christian Theology: An Introduction</u>, Malden, MA: Blackwell Publishing, 2001.

Messner, Thomas M. "Can Para church Organizations Hire and Fire on the Basis of Religion without Violating Title VII?" <u>University of Florida Journal of Law and Public Policy</u> 17, No. 1 (April 2006): 63-106

Mikolaski, Samuel J. "The Theology of the New Testament," In <u>The Expositor's Bible Commentary, Vol.1</u>, edited by Frank E. Gaebelein. Grand Rapids: Zondervan, 1979. 457-480

Morgan, Timothy C. "Re-Neighboring Our Cities," <u>Christianity Today</u> vol. 40 (January 8, 1996), 15-16.

Muck, Terry C. "Theology Colloquium: Vision Paper," <u>Mission at the Dawn of the 21st Century: A Vision For the Church,</u> edited by Paul Varo Martinson, Minneapolis: Kirk House Publishers, 1999. 219-240

Nave, Jr. Guy D. <u>The Role and Function of Repentance in Luke-Acts</u>, Atlanta: Society of Biblical Literature, 2002.

Neely, Alan. "Religious Pluralism: Threat or Opportunity for Mission?" <u>Mission at the Dawn of the 21st Century: A Vision For the Church,</u> edited by Paul Varo Martinson, Minneapolis: Kirk House Publishers, 1999. 32-47

Neusner, Jacob, Chilton, Bruce, Graham, William. <u>Three Faiths, One God</u>, Boston: Brill Academic Publishers, Inc. 2002.

Norwood, Frederick Abbott. "The Early History of the Church," In <u>The Interpreter's One Volume Commentary of the Bible</u>, Edited by Charles Layman, Nashville, TN: Abingdon Press, 1980. 1045-1053

"para-." *Dictionary.com Unabridged (v 1.1)*. Random House, Inc. 08 Oct. 2008. <Dictionary.com <u>http://dictionary.reference.com/browse/para.</u>

Payne, Claude E., Beazley, Hamilton. Reclaiming the Great Commission, San Francisco: Jossey-Bass, 2000.

Pfeiffer, Charles F. and Harrison, Everett F. The Wycliffe Bible Commentary, Chicago: Moody Press, 1990.

Porter, Lawrence B. A Guide to the Church, Staten Island, NY: the Society of St. Paul/Alba House, 2008.

"position." Encyclopedia Britannica. 2009. Encyclopedia Britannica Online. 21 Jun. 2009 <http:// www.britanica.com/EBchecked/topic/551450/social-status>

Reid, Daniel G. Concise Dictionary of Christianity in America, Eugene, OR: Wipf and Stock Publishers, 2002.

Saint Augustine. The City of God, New York: The Modern Library, 2000.

Schaller, Lyle E. The New Context for Ministry, Nashville: Abingdon Press, 2002.

Schaller, Lyle E., Tidwell, Charles A. Creative Church Administration, Nashville: Abingdon Press, 1975.

Selvanayagam, Israel. "Towards an Evangelical Theology for a Pluralist Age," Mission at the Dawn of the 21st Century: A Vision For the Church, edited by Paul Varo Martinson, Minneapolis: Kirk House Publishers, 1999.201-218

Senge, Peter M. The Fifth Discipline, New York: Doubleday Currency, 1990.

Shepherd, Jr. Massey H. "The Gospel According to John," In The Interpreter's One Volume Commentary of the Bible, Edited by Charles Layman, Nashville, TN: Abingdon Press, 1980. 707-728

Spurgeon, Charles. Being God's Friend, New Kensington, PA: Whittaker House, 1997.

Stackhouse Jr., John G. Evangelical Landscapes: Facing Critical Issues of the Day, Grand Rapids: Baker Academic, 2002.

Stafford, Tim. "When Christians Fight Christians," <u>Christianity Today</u>, vol. 41(October 6, 1997): 28-34.

Stanley, David S.J. "The Greco-Roman Background of the New Testament," In <u>The Interpreter's One Volume Commentary on the Bible</u>, Edited by Charles Layman, Nashville, TN: Abingdon Press, 1980. 1037-1044

Strong, James. <u>The New Strong's Concordance</u>, Nashville: Thomas Nelson Publishers, 1990.

Taber, Charles R. <u>To Understand the World, To Save the World</u>, Harrisburg, PA: Trinity Press International, 2000.

Taylor, Richard. <u>How to Read a Church</u>, Mahwah, NJ: Hidden Springs, 2003.

Terrien, Samuel. "The Religion of Israel," In <u>The Interpreter's One Volume Commentary of the Bible</u>, Edited by Charles Layman, Nashville, TN: Abingdon Press, 1980. 1150-1158

<u>The American Heritage Dictionary of the English Language</u> Fourth Edition, Boston MA: Houghton Mifflin Company, 2005.

<u>The Holy Bible</u>: New King James Version, Nashville: Thomas Nelson, Inc., 1994.

Thompson, Claude Holmes. "The First Letter of Peter," In <u>The Interpreter's One Volume Commentary of the Bible</u>, Edited by Charles Layman, Nashville, TN: Abingdon Press, 1980. 924-930

Tidwell, Charles A. <u>Church Administration Effective Leadership for Ministry</u>, Nashville: Broadman Press, 1985.

Townes, Elmer L. <u>Bible Answers for Almost All Your Questions</u>, Nashville: Thomas Nelson Publishers, 2003.

Vine, W.E. <u>Vine's Complete Expository Dictionary</u>, Nashville: Thomas Nelson Publishers, 1996.

Warren, Rick. <u>The Purpose Driven Church</u>, Grand Rapids: Zondervan, 1995.

Weber, Max. <u>The Protestant Ethic and the Spirit of Capitalism</u>, Chicago: Fitzroy Dearborn Publishers, 2001.

Wenham, G.J., Motyer, J.A., Carson, D. A., France, R.T. New Bible Commentary, Downers Grove, Ill.: Inter-Varsity Press, 1994.

White, Jerry. The Church and the Para church: An Uneasy Marriage, Portland: Multnomah Press, 1983.

Wilmer, Wesley K., Schmidt, J. David, Smith, Martyn. The Prospering Para church, San Francisco: Jossey-Bass Publishers, 1998.

Wilson, Jonathan R. Why Church Matters: Worship, Ministry and Mission in Practice, Grand Rapids: Brazos Press, 2006.

www.barna.org/barna-update/article/5-barna-update/182-christian-mass-media-reach-more-adults-with-the-chrisitan-message-than-do-churches.html (5/1/2009).

www.barna.org/barna-update/article/5-barna-update/182-one-in-three-adults-is-unchurched.html (5/1/2009).

Yarchin, William. History of Biblical Interpretation, Peabody, Mass: Hendrickson Publishers, 2004.

Zodhiates, Spiros. Hebrew-Greek Key Word Study Bible: New American Standard, Chattanooga, TN: AMG Publishers, 1990.